HOW TO PASS

HIGHER
MUSIC LISTENING

Joe McGowan

HODDER
GIBSON
AN HACHETTE UK COMPANY

If the CD is missing from this package, please contact us on 0141 848 1609 or at hoddergibson@hodder.co.uk, advising where and when you purchased the book.

Although every effort has been made to ensure that website addresses are correct at time of going to press, Hodder Gibson cannot be held responsible for the content of any website mentioned in this book. It is sometimes possible to find a relocated web page by typing in the address of the home page for a website in the URL window of your browser.

The publishers would like to thank Derek Norval for his assistance and advice in preparing this book.

Hachette's policy is to use papers that are natural, renewable and recyclable products and made from wood grown in sustainable forests. The logging and manufacturing processes are expected to conform to the environmental regulations of the country of origin.

Orders: please contact Bookpoint Ltd, 130 Milton Park, Abingdon, Oxon OX14 4SB. Telephone: (44) 01235 827720. Fax: (44) 01235 400454. Lines are open 9.00–5.00, Monday to Saturday, with a 24-hour message answering service. Visit our website at www.hoddereducation.co.uk. Hodder Gibson can be contacted direct on: Tel: 0141 848 1609; Fax: 0141 889 6315; email: hoddergibson@hodder.co.uk

© Joe McGowan 2007
First published in 2007 by
Hodder Gibson, an imprint of Hodder Education, an Hachette UK Company,
2a Christie Street
Paisley PA1 1NB

Impression number   5 4 3 2
Year   2010 2009

Cover photo ImageState / Alamy, ©istockphoto.com/blackred
Cartoons © Moira Munro
Typeset in 9.5 on 12.5pt Frutiger Light by Phoenix Photosetting, Chatham, Kent
Printed in Great Britain by Martins The Printers, Berwick-upon-Tweed

A catalogue record for this title is available from the British Library

ISBN-13: 978-0-340-93924-6

CONTENTS

INTRODUCTION

Welcome to another *How To Pass* book on the subject of music!

This time we are focusing on the Listening component of the Higher Music course. The reason for this is that we feel Listening is such a big part of Higher Music (and of course music in general) that it merits a book all to itself. It also seems to be an area where students feel they would benefit from as much extra help as possible. So here it is!

The exercises in this book are very similar to the questions you will encounter in the Listening question paper at the end of your course, and are structured to help you revise all the musical concepts which are unique to Higher Music, as well as those from earlier levels, in a systematic and easily digestible way. So, as you work through the book you will not only be improving your listening skills, but also gaining experience in responding to exam-style questions.

As with the other music books in the *How To Pass* series, you can use the material in the following pages for learning, practice and revision, and also as a source of reference throughout your course.

All that remains now is to wish you a 'pleasant journey' through the book, and good luck with the final Listening question paper!

HIGHER MUSIC LISTENING

The three main areas of musical activity in the Higher Music course are **Listening**, **Composing/Arranging** and **Performing**. In this section you will find details of what you are required to know for the compulsory Listening component of the course, including musical concepts new to Higher level, and the ways in which you will be assessed.

Assessment

During your Higher Music course you will learn a range of new musical concepts which will be heard in practice in a selection of prescribed reference works which you will study. The reference works will vary from time to time, but the musical concepts will remain the same.

In May of the exam year you will sit a one hour Listening question paper, based mostly on audio excerpts, involving questions relating to musical concepts and musical literacy. The audio excerpts used in this Listening question paper may include examples from the course reference works.

A total of 40 marks are available for the Listening question paper, in which there are six different question types.

Question Types in the Listening Question Paper
1. **Multiple choice**
2. **Short answers**
3. **Musical map**
4. **Musical literacy**
5. **Cloze test**
6. **Comparison of musical excerpts**

The chart on the following page gives a brief description of how you are required to respond to each question type, and also shows how the marks are distributed.

	Number of questions	Marks per question	Total marks
1. Multiple choice questions:			
◆ Select **one** correct answer from **four** options.	1	1	1
◆ Select **three** correct answers from **nine** options.	2	3	6
◆ Select **four** correct answers from **ten** options.	1	4	4
2. Short answers:			
◆ Write a few words or a phrase.	5	1	5
3. Musical map:			
◆ Describe musical devices/concepts used as they occur at specific points in a piece of music. For two of the three playings a voice will guide you through the music as you listen; this voice will be heard immediately before each point at which you should note the musical event/concept being used.	1	5	5
4. Musical literacy:			
◆ Demonstrate your technical knowledge of written music by responding to questions which require you to carry out tasks such as: rewrite a short passage of music in treble clef at the same pitch, or one or two octaves lower, in the bass clef; identify octave leaps, appoggiaturas, ornaments, etc. by placing brackets over such features where they occur in the music; insert missing notes or rests; identify incorrect rhythms and notes; complete a bar of music which has been left blank or unfinished; identify a missing time signature.	1	6	6
5. Cloze test:			
◆ Describe the music you hear by inserting the correct concepts in the appropriate places in a page of text.	1	5	5
6. Comparison of musical excerpts:			
◆ Listen to two different musical excerpts and note, from a list of possible concepts, those concepts which are present in each excerpt and those which are common to both. You will be guided to the number of concepts that you must identify in each of the three columns by the number of marks available as written at the foot of the 'Final Answer' page.	1	8	8
Total marks available			40

Note: The listening exercises in this book are all structured in the same style as the six main question types (listed on page 2) which you will encounter in the final Listening question paper. Furthermore, there is a specimen Listening question paper in Chapter 7, page 63.

New Musical Concepts at Higher Level

A selection of new concepts are introduced in Higher music which relate to all musical periods from the Renaissance to the twentieth century.

These new concepts are covered systematically throughout this book in the listening exercises, allowing you to digest a small number of concepts at a time and hear them in practice in the musical excerpts. Below is a list of the new concepts you need to understand, each listed under its appropriate category. In addition to these new concepts, you will also be expected to be completely familiar with concepts from previous levels since these will occur both in course Listening assessments and your final Listening question paper.

Definitions for all musical concepts from Access 3 level to Higher Level can be found in the Glossary of Musical Concepts, page 71.

Higher Music Concepts

MELODIC	HARMONIC	RHYTHMIC
◆ Acciaccatura	◆ Added 6th	◆ Augmentation
◆ Appoggiatura	◆ Augmented chord	◆ Diminution
◆ Harmonic and Melodic minor	◆ Diminished 7th	◆ Hemiola
◆ Microtone	◆ Diminished chord	◆ Pulse and beat; irregular metres
◆ Mode	◆ Dominant 7th	◆ Three against two
◆ Mordent	◆ Interrupted cadence	◆ Time changes
◆ Tone row	◆ Plagal cadence	
◆ Tritone	◆ Polytonality	
◆ Turn		

STRUCTURAL	TIMBRE	STYLE/FORM
◆ Antiphonal	◆ Harmonics	◆ Renaissance
◆ Basso continuo	◆ Coloratura	◆ Nationalist
◆ Bridge	◆ Sprechgesang	◆ Serial
◆ Countersubject	◆ Consort	◆ Neo-classical
◆ Episode	◆ Ripieno	◆ Late romantic
◆ Exposition	◆ Concertino	◆ Jazz-funk
◆ Inversion		◆ Musique concrète
◆ Leitmotiv		◆ Pavan
◆ Real answer		◆ Galliard
◆ Retrograde		◆ Plainchant
◆ Ritornello		◆ Mass
◆ Sonata form		◆ Motet
◆ Stretto		◆ Madrigal
◆ Subject		◆ Overture
◆ Tonal answer		◆ Sonata
◆ Transition		◆ Suite
		◆ Concerto grosso
		◆ Anthem
		◆ Air
		◆ Chant
		◆ Chorale prelude
		◆ Ballet
		◆ Chaconne/Passacaglia
		◆ Fugue
		◆ Lied
		◆ Song cycle
		◆ Symphonic/Tone poem
		◆ Da Capo aria

HOW TO USE THIS BOOK

You can work through this book in any order you please, since there is no ascending level of difficulty, but you should tackle all of the exercises as they will each help you to improve different aspects of your listening skills.

Chapters 1–6 focus on specific areas of listening relevant to the Higher Music course:

Chapter 1 deals with identifying specific chords and cadences.

Chapter 2 focuses on Renaissance music, and concepts mainly associated with this period.

Chapter 3 focuses on Baroque music, and concepts mainly associated with this period.

Chapter 4 focuses on Classical, Romantic and late Romantic music, and concepts mainly associated with these periods.

Chapter 5 focuses on twentieth-century music, and concepts mainly associated with this period.

Chapter 6 provides eight complete musical literacy exercises, together with supplementary literacy questions.

Chapter 7 is a specimen Listening question paper.

This format will allow you to focus on specific areas of the course, and so help you to acquire a more thorough knowledge and understanding of the various musical styles and concepts which are studied in Higher Music.

And don't forget, when you have eventually completed all of the exercises, the book can continue to function as a permanent source of reference, since you will effectively have a range of audio examples of the concepts you need to be familiar with (as well as definitions of each of these in the glossary).

 ## CD-based exercises

The CD which accompanies this book contains the musical excerpts for all of the listening exercises featured in chapters 1 to 7. The particular track that you need to listen to for each exercise is clearly indicated in the text.

 ## 'Hints and Tips'

Little pieces of information appear in boxes every now and then to give you helpful advice and facts on particular topics as they come up in the book.

'At a Glance' Reference Charts

These are given at the beginning of Chapters 2, 3, 4 and 5, and provide you with a brief summary of the concepts and features which are associated with the main musical styles/forms of a particular period. The purpose of these charts is to refresh your memory and help you to identify a particular musical form or style more quickly when you hear it, and also to demonstrate how making brief notes such as these can greatly assist you in the identification process. For example (from Chapter 2):

Form/Structure	Characteristic features	Period
Chant/ Plainchant/ Plainsong	Religious vocal composition associated with the early **Mass**, monasteries and the devotional singing of monks. Normally male voices. **Modal**. 'Bare' modal sounds are often created by the presence of perfect fifth intervals.	Medieval, used as a basis for some Renaissance music
Pavan	Instrumental composition. **Duple metre**. Slow to moderate **tempo**.	Renaissance
Galliard	Instrumental composition (often performed after a **pavan**). **Triple metre**. Lively **tempo**.	Renaissance
Air	Slow, simple vocal or instrumental melody/song. Airs performed by **ensembles (consorts)** or a **solo** singer **accompanied** by lute were popular, as were solo lute airs.	Renaissance

Listening Charts

Blank *Listening Charts* are given at the end of Chapters 2, 3, 4 and 5. These should be used to note down your observations about the concepts/features you hear when you listen to a particular piece of music (see example below). You might, for example, select the opening movement of a symphony from the classical period and listen to it very carefully two or three times in order to identify as many features and concepts as you can. This can be done on your own, or as a class exercise where everyone compares answers at the end of the second or third listening.

Title and Form/ Structure of Piece	Period	Concepts/Features
Beethoven's 9th symphony, first movement	Classical	* Pedal * Crescendo * Minor tonality * *sfz* chords * Modulation * Melodic sequence * Syncopation * Imitation * Staccato * Dotted rhythms * Ritardando * *a tempo* * Counterpoint * Timpani roll * Pizzicato string basses * Trill * Accelerando
Overture from *Porgy and Bess* (an opera based on jazz and gospel music)	Twentieth century	* Trill * Cymbals * Xylophone * Snare drum * Melodic sequence * Timpani * Jazz * Honky-tonk piano * Syncopation * Rubato * Chorus/choir * Scat singing * Crescendo * Ostinato

Glossary of Musical Concepts

The Glossary of Musical Concepts contains a full list of the musical concepts (complete with definitions) you need to understand at Higher level, together with those for previous levels from Access 3 to Intermediate 2 (or Foundation to Credit level in Standard Grade). The concepts are also categorised and listed in alphabetical order for easy reference.

Further Reading

Extra sources of help and reference include:

◆ **A music dictionary**. Available in bookstores and on some music websites

◆ **How To Pass Standard Grade Music** by Joe McGowan, published by Hodder Gibson. Exercises and information relating to Standard Grade music; also relevant to Access 3 and Intermediate 1 and 2 levels.

◆ **How To Pass Higher Music** by Joe McGowan, published by Hodder Gibson. Exercises and information relating to Higher level music.

Useful Websites

◆ **www.ltscotland.org.uk**
Learning and Teaching Scotland. Free downloads and information on music courses from Access 3 to Advanced Higher level

◆ **www.sqa.org.uk**
The Scottish Qualifications Authority. Up-to-date information on music courses and exam arrangements, with some free downloads available

◆ **www.liberton.edin.sch.uk**
Liberton High School. Information and audio samples relating to musical concepts studied at all levels

◆ **www.bbc.co.uk/schools/gcsebitesize**
The BBC's schools 'bitesize' website. Although dedicated to GCSE qualifications, this website contains information and audio samples which will be helpful to students studying Scottish curriculum music courses.

◆ **www.karadar.com**
Classical music dictionary. Composer biographies and music, photos, MIDI and MP3 downloads

◆ **www.digital-daydreams.com**
Various kinds of categorised information on music, including composer biographies, music history and notation

Other useful websites

The following websites exist for the purpose of promoting and selling CD recordings, but they also provide a wide range of audio samples which you can access. This will be helpful if you want to hear examples of different musical styles and concepts.

◆ **www.deutschegrammophon.com**

◆ **www.chandos-records.com**

◆ **www.wyastone.co.uk**

CHORDS AND CADENCES

At Higher level you are required to be able to identify certain chords and cadences when you hear them. This takes practice and concentration.

As in all areas of aural (or ear) training, the most effective way to improve your skills in this area is to listen to and play the chords and cadences regularly so that you eventually come to recognise the characteristic sound of each one the moment you hear it.

Part 1: Chord Identification

The six chords you need to be able to identify by ear are:

- **Added 6th chord**
- **Diminished chord**
- **Diminished 7th chord**
- **Dominant 7th chord**
- **Augmented chord**

Hints *and* Tips

Some chords are more common in certain periods than in others. For example, the more basic **modal** harmony of the Medieval and **Renaissance** periods meant that simpler chord types were used, whereas much greater harmonic experimentation in later periods (particularly the **Classical** and **Romantic** eras) saw the use of more expressive chords such as the **added 6th** and **diminished 7th**. The characteristic sounds of the **added 6th**, **diminished** and **augmented** chords are also a common feature of **twentieth-century** styles such as **jazz** and **pop** music.

Before attempting the following exercises you should play each of the above chords several times (or have them played for you) to familiarise yourself with the characteristic sound of each. Information on how each chord is constructed can be found in the Glossary of Musical Concepts (page 71).

For Practice

A really good way to develop your chord identification skills is to have someone play several sequences of between four and six chords, the last (or second-last) of which should be the chord you have to identify.

HOW TO PASS HIGHER MUSIC LISTENING

The following six listening exercises require you to identify specific chords from the list on the previous page. On each of CD tracks 1–7 you will hear a short excerpt of music in which you have to identify a particular chord.

Listening Exercise 1: CD Track 1

Listen to CD track 1. The last two chords in the excerpt form a perfect cadence (V–I). Listen very carefully to the chord that is played just before this cadence (i.e. the *third-last* chord in the excerpt, heard at *00:13*), and tick **one** box to describe it. Try to complete your answer after hearing the recorded excerpt no more than **twice**.

☐ Added 6th chord
☐ Diminished chord
☐ Diminished 7th chord
☐ Dominant 7th chord
☐ Augmented chord

Listening Exercise 2: CD Track 2

Listen to CD track 2 and tick **one** box to describe the *last* chord you hear. Try to complete your answer after hearing the recorded excerpt no more than **twice**.

☐ Added 6th chord
☐ Diminished chord
☐ Diminished 7th chord
☐ Dominant 7th chord
☐ Augmented chord

Listening Exercise 3: CD Track 3

Listen to CD track 3 and tick **one** box to describe the *last* chord you hear. Try to complete your answer after hearing the recorded excerpt no more than **twice**.

☐ Added 6th chord
☐ Diminished chord
☐ Diminished 7th chord
☐ Dominant 7th chord
☐ Augmented chord

Listening Exercise 4: CD Track 4

Listen to CD track 4 and tick **one** box to describe the *last* chord you hear. Try to complete your answer after hearing the recorded excerpt no more than **twice**.

☐ Added 6th chord
☐ Diminished chord
☐ Diminished 7th chord
☐ Dominant 7th chord
☐ Augmented chord

Listening Exercise 5: CD Track 5

Listen to CD track 5 and tick **one** box to describe the *second-last* chord you hear. Try to complete your answer after hearing the recorded excerpt no more than **twice**.

- ☐ Added 6th chord
- ☐ Diminished chord
- ☐ Diminished 7th chord
- ☐ Dominant 7th chord
- ☐ Augmented chord

Listening Exercise 6: CD Track 6

Listen to CD track 6 and tick **one** box to describe the *last* chord you hear. Try to complete your answer after hearing the recorded excerpt no more than **twice**.

- ☐ Added 6th chord
- ☐ Diminished chord
- ☐ Diminished 7th chord
- ☐ Dominant 7th chord
- ☐ Augmented chord

Part 2: Cadence Identification

The four cadences you need to be able to identify by ear are:

- ◆ **Perfect cadence**
- ◆ **Imperfect cadence**
- ◆ **Plagal cadence**
- ◆ **Interrupted cadence**

Hints *and* Tips

Here is a quick guide which you may find useful for remembering the characteristic sound of each cadence:

Perfect cadence (V – I or **IV – I)** – an 'ending' which closes a phrase on the tonic chord **I** (like a *full stop* in language).

Imperfect cadence (I – V or **I – IV)** – suggests more music is to come; keeps a phrase open (like a *comma* in language).

Plagal cadence (IV – I) – an 'ending' which closes a phrase on the tonic chord **I** and sounds like 'Amen' at the end of a hymn (like a *full stop* in language).

Interrupted cadence (V – VI) – sounds as though the music is leading to a perfect cadence but is 'interrupted' by chord **VI**, which keeps the phrase open (like a *comma* in language).

A great way to develop your cadence identification skills is to begin by playing the various cadences listed above on a harmonic instrument such as piano or keyboard to familiarise yourself with the unique sound of each, then get a fellow student to test you by playing them at random to see how many you can recognise. (Remember that the construction of each cadence can be found in the Glossary of Musical Concepts.)

HOW TO PASS HIGHER MUSIC LISTENING

The next six listening exercises require you to identify specific cadences as shown in the list on the previous page. On CD tracks 7 to 12 you will hear a short excerpt of music; you are required to identify the cadence you hear at the end of each excerpt.

Listening Exercise 7: CD Track 7

Listen to CD track 7 and tick **one** box to describe the type of cadence you hear at the end of the excerpt. Try to complete your answer after hearing the recorded excerpt no more than **twice**.

- ☐ Perfect cadence
- ☐ Imperfect cadence
- ☐ Plagal cadence
- ☐ Interrupted cadence

Listening Exercise 8: CD Track 8

Listen to CD track 8 and tick **one** box to describe the type of cadence you hear at the end of the excerpt. Try to complete your answer after hearing the recorded excerpt no more than **twice**.

- ☐ Perfect cadence
- ☐ Imperfect cadence
- ☐ Plagal cadence
- ☐ Interrupted cadence

Listening Exercise 9: CD Track 9

Listen to CD track 9 and tick **one** box to describe the type of cadence you hear at the end of the excerpt. Try to complete your answer after hearing the recorded excerpt no more than **twice**.

- ☐ Perfect cadence
- ☐ Imperfect cadence
- ☐ Plagal cadence
- ☐ Interrupted cadence

Listening Exercise 10: CD Track 10

Listen to CD track 10 and tick **one** box to describe the type of cadence you hear at the end of the excerpt. Try to complete your answer after hearing the recorded excerpt no more than **twice**.

- ☐ Perfect cadence
- ☐ Imperfect cadence
- ☐ Plagal cadence
- ☐ Interrupted cadence

Listening Exercise 11: CD Track 11

Listen to CD track 11 and tick **one** box to describe the type of cadence you hear at the end of the excerpt. Try to complete your answer after hearing the recorded excerpt no more than **twice**.

- ☐ Perfect cadence
- ☐ Imperfect cadence
- ☐ Plagal cadence
- ☐ Interrupted cadence

Listening Exercise 12: CD Track 12

Listen to CD track 12 and tick **one** box to describe the type of cadence you hear at the end of the excerpt. Try to complete your answer after hearing the recorded excerpt no more than **twice**.

- ☐ Perfect cadence
- ☐ Imperfect cadence
- ☐ Plagal cadence
- ☐ Interrupted cadence

CHORDS AND CADENCES

RENAISSANCE MUSIC

Before the Renaissance, the 'Middle Ages' or Medieval period lasted from the fifth to the fifteenth century, but owing to the fact that there was no reliable system of notating music until at least the ninth century, 'Medieval music' normally indicates music from about the eleventh to the fifteenth century.

Typical music of the Medieval period includes religious **vocal** works such as the **chant** – of which the famous *Gregorian chant* is an example – and the **mass**. Both **syllabic** and **melismatic** singing were employed, and all of the music was **modal** since tonal music (music which uses keys) had not been developed at the time.

The era in history which lasted from around 1430 to the end of the sixteenth century was known as the Renaissance period. The word *renaissance* means 're-birth', and refers to the intellectual ideal of the time which sought to revive the artistic, intellectual and philosophical principles of ancient Greece and Rome, and reject those of the previous (Medieval) era.

The Renaissance saw several musical innovations and new styles emerge, including the **chanson**, **motet**, **madrigal**, **galliard, pavan** and instrumental and vocal **consort** music, and because printing was invented in Europe during this era, music could also be published and circulated more freely.

Imitative polyphony is a characteristic style of Renaissance music. Two of the most popular instruments of the time were the **lute** and the **recorder**.

Famous composers of the period include Palestrina, Dowland, Byrd and Lassus.

Musical concepts associated with the Renaissance period

As this chapter focuses on **Renaissance** music, many of the concepts you need to know about for the listening exercises which follow are particularly associated with this musical era – but be aware that certain concepts (such as **mass**, **motet**, **anthem** and **hemiola**) may also be found in music from other periods.

Note: Concepts from previous grades are also used in all of the following exercises, and you will therefore need to have a good knowledge of them before starting your listening work here. Definitions of these musical concepts and those from Higher level appear in the Glossary of Musical Concepts on page 71, and additional listening exercises can be found in the books *How To Pass Higher Music* and *How To Pass Standard Grade Music*, published by Hodder Gibson.

Listed below are the Higher Music concepts associated with Renaissance music. Before attempting listening exercises 13–20 make sure you fully understand the meaning of each of these concepts and are confident in your ability to recognise them by ear. You may find the *'At a glance' Listening Reference Chart* on the following pages handy for refreshing your memory, but you might also find it helpful to jot down a little information of your own about each concept to jog your memory before you begin.

- air
- anthem
- antiphonal
- ballett
- chant/plainchant/plainsong
- consort
- galliard

- hemiola
- madrigal
- mass
- mode
- motet
- pavan
- Renaissance

'At a Glance' Listening Reference Chart

Form/Structure	Characteristic features	Period
Chant/ Plainchant/ Plainsong	Religious vocal composition associated with the early **mass**, monasteries and the devotional singing of monks. Male voices. **Modal**. 'Bare' modal sounds are often created by the presence of perfect fifth intervals.	Medieval, used as a basis for some Renaissance music.
Pavan	Instrumental composition. **Duple metre**. Slow to moderate **tempo**.	Renaissance
Galliard	Instrumental composition (often performed after a **pavan**). **Triple metre**. Lively tempo.	Renaissance
Air	Slow, simple vocal or instrumental **melody/song**. **Airs** performed by **ensembles** or a **solo** singer **accompanied** by lute were popular, as were solo lute airs.	Renaissance
Ballett	Non-religious vocal composition, similar to a **madrigal** but more lively and dance-like. A concert piece, **strophic**, with a *fa-la* **chorus**.	Renaissance
Madrigal	Normally a non-religious vocal piece for several voices, sometimes with instrumental **accompaniment**. Madrigals typically include **polyphony**, **imitative polyphony** and **word painting**.	Renaissance
Mass	Large-scale religious vocal composition based on the Roman Catholic Mass Service. Main sections of the mass are: Kyrie, Gloria, Credo, Sanctus Benedictus, Agnus Dei, Benedicamus Domino – these words are sung in each corresponding section of the mass. Concepts which can be used in masses: **chants**, **melismatic word setting**, **polyphony**. Developed from early **chants/plainsong**.	Medieval and Renaissance

Form/Structure	Characteristic features	Period
Anthem	Short choral composition with a religious or moral theme associated with Church of England religious services. English text. Concepts which can be used in anthems: vocal **imitation** or vocal **counterpoint**, **choruses**, **soloists**, **organ accompaniment**, **homophony**. With greater variety in vocal texture and instrumental accompaniment, the anthem often sounds slightly less 'serious' than the **mass**.	Renaissance
Motet	Normally a religious vocal composition. Early motet structure: slow-moving vocal part over which two or three faster-moving upper voices sang. Later, in the Renaissance, up to six individual parts were used. Concepts which can be used in motets: **polyphony**, **imitative polyphony/counterpoint**. Later **Baroque motets** could also include instrumental parts and **continuo accompaniment**.	Medieval and Renaissance

Hints and Tips

When you have to identify, from a list, a number of concepts present in a musical excerpt (in Listening question papers, for example), rather than trying to listen for *specific* concepts from the list during the first listening, you may find it helpful to make a quick note of the *obvious* features you hear in the music, then compare this with the options on the question paper. Any features from your notes which match those on the question paper will be correct answers. Another method is to begin by eliminating from the list those features which you think are definitely *not* present, leaving you with a shorter list of possible correct answers.

The following six listening exercises are multiple choice questions where you have to identify three features/concepts from a list of nine.

Listening Exercise 13: CD Track 13

Read through the list of features below very carefully before listening to CD track 13. Try to complete your answer after hearing the recorded excerpt no more than **twice**.

Listen to CD track 13 and tick **three** boxes to identify features present in the music.

- ☐ Madrigal
- ☐ Air
- ☐ Motet
- ☐ Anthem
- ☐ Melismatic word setting
- ☐ Chromatic notes
- ☐ Syncopation
- ☐ Ballett
- ☐ Hemiola

Listening Exercise 14: CD Track 14
Read through the list of features below very carefully before listening to CD track 14. Try to complete your answer after hearing the recorded excerpt no more than **twice**.

Listen to CD track 14 and tick **three** boxes to identify features present in the music.

☐ Antiphonal   ☐ Imitative polyphony

☐ Hymn tune   ☐ Melismatic word setting

☐ Anthem   ☐ Anacrusis

☐ Madrigal   ☐ Tierce de Picardie

☐ Motet

Listening Exercise 15: CD Track 15
Read through the list of features below very carefully before listening to CD track 15. Try to complete your answer after hearing the recorded excerpt no more than **twice**.

Listen to CD track 15 and tick **three** boxes to identify features present in the music.

☐ Pizzicato   ☐ Major tonality

☐ Pavan   ☐ Accelerando

☐ Galliard   ☐ Imitation

☐ Minor tonality   ☐ Hemiola

☐ Consort

Listening Exercise 16: CD Track 16
Read through the list of features below very carefully before listening to CD track 16. Try to complete your answer after hearing the recorded excerpt no more than **twice**.

Listen to CD track 16 and tick **three** boxes to identify features present in the music.

☐ Rallentando   ☐ Modulation

☐ Syllabic word setting   ☐ Ballett

☐ Triple metre (3/4 time)   ☐ Through-composed

☐ Variation   ☐ Homophony

☐ Syncopation

Listening Exercise 17: CD Track 17
Read the question and the features below very carefully before listening to CD track 17. Try to complete your answer after hearing the recorded excerpt no more than **twice**.

Listen to CD track 17 and tick **three** boxes to identify features present in the music.

☐ Staccato   ☐ Melismatic word setting

☐ Ballett   ☐ Plagal cadence

☐ Consort   ☐ Accelerando

☐ Mass   ☐ Polyphony

☐ Plainchant

Listening Exercise 18: CD Track 18

Read the question and the features below very carefully before listening to CD track 18. Try to complete your answer after hearing the recorded excerpt no more than **twice**.

Listen to CD track 18 and tick **three** boxes to identify features present in the music.

☐ Tierce de Picardie   ☐ Consort

☐ Triple metre (3/4)   ☐ Quadruple metre (4/4)

☐ Accelerando   ☐ Glissando

☐ Galliard   ☐ Pavan

☐ Pizzicato

The final two listening exercises in this chapter are multiple choice questions where you have to identify four features/concepts from a list of ten.

Listening Exercise 19: CD Track 19

Read the question and the features below very carefully before listening to CD track 19. Try to complete your answer after hearing the recorded excerpt no more than **three times**.

Listen to CD track 19 and tick **four** boxes to identify features present in the music.

☐ Plainchant   ☐ Hemiola

☐ Consort   ☐ Legato

☐ Antiphonal   ☐ Suspension

☐ Hymn tune   ☐ Mode

☐ Motet   ☐ Air

Listening Exercise 20: CD Track 20

Read the question and the features below very carefully before listening to CD track 20. Try to complete your answer after hearing the recorded excerpt no more than **three times**.

Listen to CD track 20 and tick **four boxes** to identify features present in the music.

☐ Ballett   ☐ Motet

☐ Word painting   ☐ Polyphony

☐ Trill   ☐ Syllabic word setting

☐ Descant   ☐ Rallentando

☐ Hemiola   ☐ Consort

For Practice

On pages 19 and 20 there is a Renaissance Music Listening Chart for you to note down your observations as you listen to recordings (chosen by you or your teacher) of the various musical styles from these periods.

For extra guidance, see How to Use This Book, page 6.

Renaissance Music Listening Chart

Title	Form/ Structure	Concepts/Features
	Chant/Plainchant/ Plainsong	
	Pavan	
	Galliard	
	Air	
	Ballett	

Title	Form/ Structure	Concepts/Features
	Madrigal	
	Mass	
	Anthem	
	Motet	

BAROQUE MUSIC

In musical history, the period lasting between approximately 1600 and 1750 was known as the Baroque era.

Characteristic features of Baroque music include **contrast** in **texture**, **dynamics** and **tempo** (which was a significant move away from the music of the previous Renaissance period), and the use of the **basso continuo**.

Several important new styles/forms also emerged. In instrumental music these included the **concerto grosso**, **chorale prelude**, **fugue**, **chaconne**, **passacaglia**, **French and Italian overtures,** and the **suite**; and in vocal music the **da capo aria**, **cantata**, **passion** and **oratorio**.

Among the famous Baroque composers were Monteverdi, Corelli, Vivaldi, Handel and J S Bach.

Musical concepts associated with the Baroque period

As this chapter focuses on **Baroque** music, many of the concepts you need to know about for the listening exercises which follow are particularly associated with this musical era – but be aware that certain concepts may also be found in music from other periods.

Before attempting exercises 21–29 make sure you fully understand the meaning of each of the Higher Music concepts below and are confident in your ability to recognise them by ear; the same applies for concepts from previous grades which also appear in the exercises. (Remember that it might help to write down a little about each concept in order to jog your memory before you begin.)

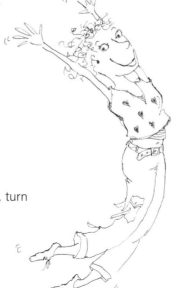

- augmentation
- basso continuo
- chaconne/passacaglia
- concertino
- concerto grosso
- da capo aria
- diminution
- overture
- fugue
- ornaments: acciaccatura, appoggiatura, mordent, turn
- real answer
- ripieno
- ritornello
- suite
- tonal answer

'At a Glance' Listening Reference Chart

Style/Form/Concept	Characteristic features	Period
Concerto grosso	Instrumental composition. Unlike later concertos, the structure is not solo instrument and orchestra, but **concertino** (small group of instruments) and **ripieno** or **concerto grosso** (large group of instruments). The two groups create **contrasting** sounds and **dynamics**: often a 'bigger' sound with the ripieno, and a more delicate sound with the concertino (it can sound like a musical conversation between the two groups). **Continuo** also used.	Baroque
Chaconne/Passacaglia	Instrumental dances based on **variation** form. **Ground bass** frequently used.	Baroque
Fugue	Instrumental composition based on **imitation**. The first **theme**, the **subject**, is imitated by another part, the **answer**. A **real answer** is an accurate note-for-note repeat of the subject, usually in the **dominant** key. A **tonal answer** is one where certain notes are altered to fit harmonically with the other parts. The second theme, the **countersubject**, begins when the answer is playing. This overlapping texture creates **counterpoint**. In between repeats of subject and answer themes are small sections called **episodes**.	Baroque/Classical
Da capo aria	Vocal composition in **ternary** form (ABA). A and B sections contain contrasting music. At the end of the B section the instruction '**Da capo**' (go back to the beginning) is given, meaning the A section is repeated.	Baroque/Classical
Suite	A collection of short instrumental pieces intended to be played in a particular order and in a single performance, collectively forming a large single work. Typically the pieces were all dances in the same key, but each with a different character, **tempo** and **metre**. The common dances were *bourée*, *allemande*, *courante*, *sarabande*, *minuet* and *gigue*.	Baroque
Overture	A large scale instrumental work. The *French overture* is characterised by an opening section in **duple metre** and a slow to moderate **tempo** (where **dotted rhythms** feature), followed by a faster second section in **triple metre** or **compound time** (and sometimes returning again to the slow speed before the end). The *Italian overture*, or *sinfonia*, is based on a three-section fast-slow-fast structure in which the trumpet often has an important role. In later **Classical** music, the **overture** was often used as an introduction to an **opera**, where themes from the opera itself might be included in this instrumental piece.	Baroque

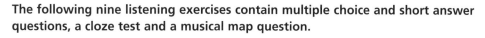

BAROQUE MUSIC

The following nine listening exercises contain multiple choice and short answer questions, a cloze test and a musical map question.

Listening Exercise 21: CD Track 21

This exercise features music by Corelli.

Read through the features below very carefully before listening to CD track 21. Try to answer part (a) after hearing the recorded excerpt no more than **three times**.

(a) Listen to CD track 21 and tick **four** boxes to identify features present in the music.

☐ Basso continuo   ☐ Diminution

☐ Concerto grosso   ☐ Perfect cadence

☐ Passacaglia   ☐ Diminished chord

☐ Modulation   ☐ Tierce de Picardie

☐ Overture   ☐ Pizzicato

Listen to CD track 21 again and answer questions (b) and (c). Try to complete your answers after listening to the excerpt again no more than **twice**.

(b) Name the musical ornament (other than a trill) which forms part of the main melody from about halfway through the excerpt (*0:23*) to the end.

(c) In this style/form of piece, a main group of players and a smaller solo group was a typical feature. What was the name given to (i) the large group and (ii) the smaller solo group?

(i) The large group was known as the:

(ii) The smaller solo group was known as the:

Listening Exercise 22: CD Track 22

Read through the features below very carefully before listening to CD track 22. Try to complete your answers after hearing the recorded excerpt no more than **three** times.

Listen to CD track 22 and tick **four boxes** to identify features present in the music.

☐ Passion   ☐ Suspension

☐ Tierce de Picardie   ☐ Antiphonal

☐ Trill   ☐ Interrupted cadence

☐ Turn   ☐ A cappella

☐ Homophony   ☐ Da Capo Aria

Listening Exercise 23: CD Track 23

Read through the features on the following page very carefully before listening to CD track 23. Try to answer part (a) after hearing the recorded excerpt no more than **three** times.

(a) Listen to CD track 23 and tick **four** boxes to identify features present in the music.

☐ Overture   ☐ Tremolando/tremolo

☐ Ground bass   ☐ Chaconne

☐ Mode   ☐ Acciaccatura

☐ Drone bass/pedal   ☐ Dotted rhythms

☐ Trill   ☐ Cadenza

Listen to CD track 23 again and answer questions (b) and (c). Try to complete your answers after listening to the excerpt again no more than **twice**.

(b) About two-thirds of the way through the excerpt, the music changes and becomes livelier. Listen to CD track 23 again and tick **one** box to describe an important feature of this change.

☐ The time signature changes from simple time to compound time

☐ The time signature changes from compound time to simple time

☐ Hemiola

☐ The time signature changes from 4/4 time to 2/4 time

(c) Name the percussion instrument used in the excerpt.
☐

Listening Exercise 24: CD Track 24

Read through the features below very carefully before listening to CD track 24. Try to answer part (a) after hearing the recorded excerpt no more than **three** times.

(a) Listen to CD track 24 and tick **four** boxes to describe features present in the music.

☐ Overture   ☐ Syncopation

☐ Chorale prelude   ☐ Ritornello

☐ Triplets   ☐ Augmented chord

☐ Mordent   ☐ Countermelody

☐ Tierce de Picardie   ☐ Glissando

Listen to CD track 24 again and answer questions (b) and (c). Try to complete your answers after listening to the excerpt again no more than **twice**.

(b) Name the keyboard instrument playing the music. ☐

(c) Name another keyboard instrument which was popular in the Baroque period.
☐

Listening Exercise 25: CD Track 25

Read through the features on the following page very carefully before listening to CD track 25. Try to complete your answers after hearing the recorded excerpt no more than **three** times.

Listen to CD track 25 and tick **four** boxes to identify features present in the music.

☐ Alberti bass   ☐ Walking bass

☐ Modulation   ☐ Rallentando

☐ Transition   ☐ Triplets

☐ Plagal cadence   ☐ Basso continuo

☐ Minuet   ☐ Diminished chord

Listening Exercise 26: CD Tracks 26 and 27
This exercise features music by J S Bach.

Read through the features below very carefully before listening to CD track 26. Try to answer part (a) after hearing the recorded excerpt no more than **three** times.

(a) Listen to CD track 26 and tick **four** boxes to describe features present in the music.

☐ Countersubject   ☐ Augmentation

☐ Overture   ☐ Stretto

☐ Answer   ☐ Fugue

☐ Chaconne   ☐ Inverted pedal

☐ Chorale prelude   ☐ Ground bass

CD Track 27. Listen to CD track 27 and answer questions (b), (c) and (d). Try to complete your answers after listening to the excerpt no more than **three** times.

(b) Describe the tonality.

(c) The music is performed by a duet of the same type of musical instrument. Name this instrument.

(d) Tick **one** box to describe a structural feature of the music.

☐ Obbligato

☐ Pedal

☐ Canon

☐ Basso continuo

Hints and Tips

The following exercise is a **Cloze Test**. In this type of listening exercise you are required to insert the correct concepts in the appropriate places in a passage of text.

A good way to approach this type of exercise is to read through the passage very carefully first of all, just to give yourself an idea of the kinds of concepts you will be expected to insert, before listening to the excerpt for the first time. Don't be tempted to race through the text trying to insert each concept as you listen to the music, but instead just try to get an overall feel for the music during the first listening, inserting only those concepts which are obvious to you. On subsequent listenings, you will become more familiar with the music and therefore better able to focus on specific areas of the text.

Listening Exercise 27: CD Track 28

In this exercise you will describe the music you hear by inserting the correct concepts in the appropriate places in the text below.

Read through the text below very carefully before listening to CD track 28. Try to complete your answers after hearing the recorded excerpt no more than **three** times.

The excerpt opens with _____ playing a melody which begins not on the first beat of the bar, but with an _____. One of the accompanying instruments is cello, which sometimes can be heard repeating the same bass note to create a _____. Also accompanying is a harpsichord; this instrument was often used as an accompaniment instrument in Baroque music in a part of the orchestra known as the _____. After a section where a second melodic idea or theme is played, and then repeated, there follows a passage played by solo violins. Two ornaments used by the violins in this passage are an _____ and a _____. Another technique is used where the violinists, instead of changing the bow direction for each note, play two or more notes with a single up-bow or down-bow. This common string technique is known as _____. When the solo violin passage is finished, the larger instrumental group or full orchestra enter again, repeating one of the melodic themes played earlier. This particular melodic theme is repeated several times throughout the piece by the main instrumental group and is known as a _____. The style/form of the piece is a _____.

Listening Exercise 28: CD Track 29

Read through the features below very carefully before listening to CD track 29. Try to answer part (a) after hearing the recorded excerpt no more than **three times**.

(a) Listen to CD track 29 and tick **four** boxes to describe features present in the music.

☐ Rallentando	☐ Plainchant
☐ Chorale prelude	☐ Oratorio
☐ Da capo aria	☐ Triplets
☐ Antiphonal	☐ Alberti bass
☐ Perfect cadence	☐ A capella

CD Track 29. Listen to CD track 29 again and answer questions (b), (c) and (d). Try to complete your answers after listening to the excerpt no more than **three** times.

(b) (i)   Which brass instrument plays solo in the music?

(ii) Which percussion instrument is used?

(c) Describe a rhythmic feature which closely unites the solo brass instrument and the percussion instrument towards the end of the excerpt.

(d) Tick **one** box to describe a feature of the singing.

☐ Homophonic SATB   ☐ Trill

☐ Sprechgesang   ☐ Descant

Listening Exercise 29: CD Track 30

This excerpt comes from Handel's Coronation Anthem *Zadok the Priest*. A 'musical map' of the excerpt is laid out below; read the question very carefully before listening to CD track 30. As you can see, you are required to insert information in the highlighted areas **1–4**. A voice will guide you through the excerpt as you listen. This voice will be heard immediately before the music for each of the highlighted areas is heard. Try to complete this exercise after listening to the excerpt no more than **three times**.

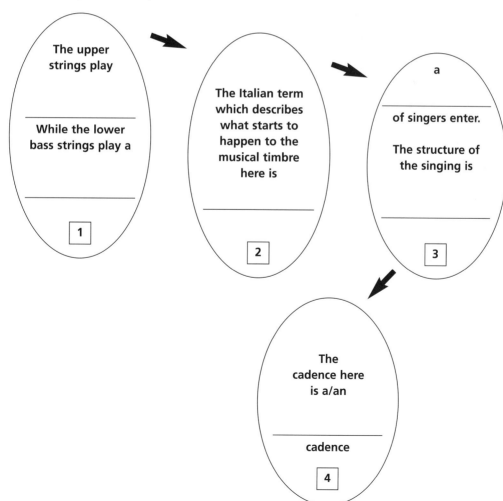

For Practice

On pages 28 and 29 there is a Baroque Music Listening Chart for you to note down your observations as you listen to recordings (chosen by you or your teacher) of the various musical styles from this period. For extra guidance, see How to Use This Book, page 6.

Baroque Music Listening Chart

Title	Form/ Structure	Concepts/Features
	Chaconne	
	Passacaglia	
	Concerto grosso	
	Da capo aria	

Title	Form/ Structure	Concepts/Features
	Overture	
	Fugue	
	Suite	

CLASSICAL AND ROMANTIC MUSIC

Classical music

From around 1750 to 1790 the Classical period existed, an era rich in new musical developments, the most significant of which were **sonata** form and the **symphony**.

The biggest influence on Classical music (and indeed on all the art forms of this period) was the preoccupation with symmetry and proportion, which gave rise to **sonata** form. Instrumental sonatas for small forces were popular, but sonata form was also used in the construction of large scale works such as **concertos** and **symphonies**. Key **modulations** and orchestral 'colour' were also very important in Classical music, as was the **development** of musical **themes**.

Famous Classical composers include Haydn, Mozart, and Beethoven.

Romantic and late Romantic music

Following the Classical period, from about 1790 to 1910 the Romantic and late Romantic eras reigned.

Aspects such as symmetry, structure and balance became looser in Romantic music than they had been in the preceding Classical period – the driving influences now being emotion, fantasy, romance and the expression of imagination. As a result, styles such as the **symphonic poem**, the piano miniature and the **song cycle** emerged.

Romantic composers include Wagner, Chopin, Liszt and Schubert.

Musical concepts associated with the Classical, Romantic and late Romantic periods

In this chapter, most of the musical concepts you need to know about are particularly associated with **Classical**, **Romantic** and **late Romantic** music, but be aware that certain concepts may also be found in music from other periods.

Before attempting exercises 30–41 make sure you fully understand the meaning of each of the Higher Music concepts below and are confident in your ability to recognise them by ear; the same applies for concepts from previous levels which also appear in the exercises. (Remember that it might help to write down a little about each concept in order to jog your memory before you begin.)

- bridge
- coloratura
- exposition
- harmonics
- late Romantic
- leitmotiv
- lied
- nationalist
- sonata
- sonata form
- song cycle
- stretto
- symphonic/tone poem
- three against two
- transition

'At a Glance' Listening Reference Chart

Style/Form/Concept	Characteristic features	Period
Nationalist	Music which in some way reflects the nationality of a country or a composer. Traditional folk melodies, dance rhythms and instruments might be used.	Romantic/Late Romantic
Late Romantic	Normally very expressive, dramatic and emotional. Different kinds of percussion instruments are frequently used. Brass instruments important in the symphony orchestra. Can often sound like incidental music for an action film! Loose musical structures.	Approx. 1890–1910
Sonata/sonata form	Important form for Classical instrumental music. The structure is: **exposition** (which introduces the main **themes**; these are divided into first subject and second subject, are in different keys, and are separated by a **transition** or **bridge** passage and concluded by a brief **coda**); **development** (which develops the exposition material by repeating it with **variation** and in different keys) and **recapitulation** (which repeats the exposition material but with the second subject now in the tonic key).	Mainly classical, but also Romantic
Symphonic/tone poem	A large-scale orchestral work based on a particular story, poem or event which is expressed in the music alone. The music is normally highly expressive and emotional.	Romantic/Late Romantic
Lied	(German for 'song'.) An art song, normally for solo voice accompanied by piano. Common concepts used in Lieder (the plural of Lied) are: **ternary** structure, **strophic**, **melismatic** and **syllabic** word setting.	Romantic/Late Romantic
Song cycle	A group or 'cycle' of songs which are united by a common theme, although each song is complete in itself.	Romantic/Late Romantic
Transition	A linking passage which smoothly joins two main themes or sections of music together – often using a key **modulation**.	Classical onwards
Bridge	A short linking passage. In Classical music, has a similar function to a **transition** passage; in modern songs a bridge may be used to join a verse to the chorus.	Classical onwards
Exposition	The opening section of a piece in **sonata** form, where the main **themes** are introduced.	Classical onwards
Coloratura	A florid, ornamented kind of vocal technique where a passage of music is 'decorated' with flourishes of different notes (often spanning a wide range) by the singer.	Classical

CLASSICAL AND ROMANTIC MUSIC

The following twelve listening exercises contain multiple choice and short answer questions, as well as a comparison of musical excerpts question.

Listening Exercise 30: CD Track 31
Read through the features below very carefully before listening to CD track 31. Try to answer part (a) after hearing the recorded excerpt no more than **three times**.

(a) On CD track 31 you will hear an excerpt from the opening of a piano sonata. Listen to the track and tick **four** boxes to identify features present in the music.

☐ Trill   ☐ Harmonic sequence

☐ Melodic sequence   ☐ Triple metre

☐ Glissando   ☐ Late Romantic

☐ Note clusters   ☐ Ritardando

☐ Discord   ☐ Alberti bass

Listen to CD track 31 again and answer questions (b) and (c). Try to complete your answers after listening to the excerpt again no more than **twice**.

(b) What is this opening section of a piece of music in sonata form called?

(c) Two kinds of cadence occur in main areas of the music; one just before the middle of the excerpt and one at the end. Name both of these cadences.

    (i) **Cadence 1** (0:18)

    (ii) **Cadence 2** (at end of excerpt)

Listening Exercise 31: CD Tracks 32 and 33
Read through the features below very carefully before listening to CD track 32. Try to answer part (a) after hearing the recorded excerpt no more than **three** times.

(a) On CD track 32 you will hear an excerpt from an instrumental trio. Listen to the track and tick **four** boxes to describe features present in the music.

☐ Acciaccatura   ☐ Chamber music

☐ Melodic sequence   ☐ Rubato

☐ Arpeggio   ☐ Anacrusis

☐ Appoggiatura   ☐ Repetition

☐ Modulation   ☐ Syncopation

Listen to CD track 32 again and answer questions (b) and (c). Try to complete your answers after listening to the excerpt again no more than **twice**.

(b) The music is in compound time. State the metre (or time signature).

(c) Name the three instruments which play this trio.

1. [ ]

2. [ ]

3. [ ]

CD Track 33. On CD track 33 you will hear a continuation of the music from track 32. Read through the features below very carefully before listening to CD track 33. Try to answer part (a) after hearing the recorded excerpt no more than **three** times.

(a) Listen to CD track 33 and tick **four** boxes to identify features present in the music.

☐ Diminished 7th chord ☐ Three against two

☐ Inverted pedal ☐ Acciaccatura

☐ Stretto ☐ Harmonics

☐ Chromatic notes ☐ Syncopation

☐ Imitation ☐ Ground bass

Listen to CD track 33 again and answer questions (b), (c) and (d). Try to complete your answers after listening to the excerpt again no more than **twice**.

(b) What type of cadence does the excerpt end with? [ ]

(c) In which musical period (Classical, Romantic or late Romantic) was this piece written?

[ ]

(d) Tick **one** box to describe another feature present.

☐ Alberti bass

☐ Modulation

☐ Accelerando

☐ Vamp

Listening Exercise 32: CD Track 34

Read through the features below very carefully before listening to CD track 34. Try to answer part (a) after hearing the recorded excerpt no more than **twice**.

(a) Listen to CD track 34 and tick **three boxes** to identify features present in the music.

☐ Tremolando/tremolo ☐ Imitation

☐ Staccato ☐ Trill

☐ Interrupted cadence ☐ Hemiola

☐ Through-composed ☐ Augmented chord

☐ Crescendo

Listen to CD track 34 again and answer questions (b), (c) and (d). Try to complete your answers after listening to the excerpt again no more than **twice**.

(b) At the start of the excerpt, various instruments play staggered entries of the same music, in a kind of overlapping imitation. Name the concept which best describes this technique.

⬚

(c) (i) From which type of instrumental composition is the excerpt taken?

⬚

(ii) From which musical period (Classical or late Romantic) does the excerpt come?

⬚

(d) Tick **one** box to describe a feature of the style of the music.

☐ March

☐ Minuet

☐ Scherzo

☐ Waltz

Listening Exercise 33: CD Track 35
This exercise features music by Debussy.

Read through the features below very carefully before listening to CD track 35. Try to complete your answer after hearing the recorded excerpt no more than **three** times.

Listen to CD track 35 and tick **four boxes** to identify features present in the music.

☐ Chromatic notes   ☐ Note row

☐ Microtone   ☐ Bending

☐ Imitation   ☐ Pedal

☐ Impressionism   ☐ Tritone

☐ Ostinato   ☐ Syncopation

Listening Exercise 34: CD Track 36
This exercise features solo piano music.

Read through the features below very carefully before listening to CD track 36. Try to complete your answer after hearing the recorded excerpt no more than **three** times.

Listen to CD track 36 and tick **four boxes** to identify features present in the music.

☐ Accelerando   ☐ Acciaccatura

☐ Broken chords   ☐ Modal

☐ Staccato   ☐ Dominant 7th chord

☐ Repetition   ☐ Cadenza

☐ Sonata   ☐ Rhythmic ostinato

Listening Exercise 35: CD Track 37

Read through the features below very carefully before listening to CD track 37. Try to answer part (a) after hearing the recorded excerpt no more than **three** times.

(a) Listen to CD track 37 and tick **four boxes** to describe features present in the music.

☐ Recitative ☐ Coloratura

☐ Timpani ☐ Staccato

☐ Plagal cadence ☐ Augmentation

☐ Aria ☐ Three against two

☐ Leitmotiv ☐ Diminished chord

Listen to CD track 37 again and answer questions (b), (c) and (d). Try to complete your answers after listening to the excerpt again no more than **twice**.

(b) From which type of vocal composition is the excerpt taken?

(c) What type of cadence is played by the orchestral strings at both *0:22* and *1:01* in the excerpt?

(d) Tick **one** box to describe the musical style.

☐ Classical

☐ Symphonic/tone poem

☐ Romantic

☐ Late Romantic

Listening Exercise 36: CD Track 38

Read the question and the features below very carefully before listening to CD track 38. Try to answer part (a) after hearing the recorded excerpt no more than **three** times.

(a) Listen to CD track 38 and tick **four boxes** to describe features present in the music.

☐ Alberti bass ☐ Vibrato

☐ Descending chromatic scale ☐ Ascending chromatic scale

☐ Interrupted cadence ☐ Col legno

☐ Trill ☐ Note clusters

☐ Staccato ☐ Tremolando/tremolo

Listen to CD track 38 again and answer questions (b) and (c). Try to complete your answers after listening to the excerpt again no more than **twice**.

(b) From which type of composition is the excerpt taken?

(c) Tick **one** box to describe a feature present in the solo instrument.

☐ Contrary motion

☐ Double stopping

☐ Dotted rhythms

☐ Triplets

Hints and Tips

The next exercise is a **Comparison of Musical Excerpts** question in which you will listen to two different excerpts of music and, from a list of possible concepts, select those which are present in each excerpt, and those which are common to both. You are required to note two concepts which are present in Excerpt 1, three concepts which are present in Excerpt 2, and three concepts which are common to both excerpts.

You are provided with a grid for your rough working (GRID 1), and you should make full use of this before inserting your final answers in GRID 2.

On the first hearing of each excerpt, try to enter the most obvious concepts first, such as the musical style/form of each excerpt, together with any other obvious features you note. You are likely to hear other features as you become more familiar with the excerpts on subsequent playings, and will therefore be able to indentify more concepts which may not have been obvious on the first hearing.

Don't waste time thinking about which concepts are common to both excerpts while you are listening to them; these will be obvious when you compare your answers for Excerpt 1 and Excerpt 2 in your rough working grid (GRID 1).

Listening Exercise 37: CD Tracks 39 and 40

CD Tracks 39 and 40. You will now compare two excerpts of vocal music. Listed in the **left** column of the answer pages which follow are a range of musical concepts. From that column you should select features which are present in the excerpts by placing a tick in the appropriate column (**EXCERPT 1, EXCERPT 2, COMMON TO BOTH EXCERPTS**). The number of marks given at the bottom of each column in **[GRID 2] FINAL ANSWER** indicates the maximum number of concepts that should be ticked in that column.

Read the list of concepts (in column 1) carefully before listening to CD track 39 (EXCERPT 1) and CD track 40 (EXCERPT 2), and tick the musical concepts in each piece under the headings given in **[GRID 1]**. **This is your rough work**.

After listening to each excerpt no more than **three times** you should put your final answers in **[GRID 2]**.

[GRID 1] ROUGH WORKING ONLY

CONCEPTS	EXCERPT 1 (CD track 39)	EXCERPT 2 (CD track 40)	COMMON TO BOTH EXCERPTS
TIMBRE Col legno			
Coloratura			
Sprechgesang			
Bass voice			
Tenor voice			
HARMONIC Interrupted cadence			
Modulation			
Suspension			
Diminished 7th chord			
Major tonality			
STRUCTURAL Inverted pedal			
Compound time			
Alberti bass			
Through-composed			
Rhythmic ostinato			
STYLES/FORMS Recitative			
Cantata			
Aria			
Lied			
Opera			

[GRID 2] FINAL ANSWER

CONCEPTS	EXCERPT 1 (CD track 39)	EXCERPT 2 (CD track 40)	COMMON TO BOTH EXCERPTS
TIMBRE Col legno			
Coloratura			
Sprechgesang			
Bass voice			
Tenor voice			
HARMONIC Interrupted cadence			
Modulation			
Suspension			
Diminished 7th chord			
Major tonality			
STRUCTURAL Inverted pedal			
Compound time			
Alberti bass			
Through-composed			
Rhythmic ostinato			
STYLES/FORMS Recitative			
Cantata			
Aria			
Lied			
Opera			
	2 marks	3 marks	3 marks

Listening Exercise 38: CD Track 41

This question is based on an extract from Tchaikovsky's *Romeo and Juliet*, which was inspired by Shakespeare's famous play of the same name.

Read through the features below very carefully before listening to CD track 41. Try to answer part (a) after hearing the recorded excerpt no more than **twice**.

(a) Listen to CD track 41 and tick **three boxes** to identify features present in the music.

☐ Triplets   ☐ Legato

☐ Timpani   ☐ Ground bass

☐ Symphonic/Tone poem   ☐ Pizzicato

☐ Augmented chord   ☐ Harmonics

☐ Whole tone scale

Listen to CD track 41 again and answer questions (b) and (c). Try to complete your answers after listening to the excerpt again no more than **twice**.

(b) Which brass instrument plays a descending harmonic sequence at the beginning of the excerpt?

(c) Name two woodwind instruments which play **solo** melodic parts.

(i)

(ii)

Listening Exercise 39: CD Track 42

This exercise is based on an excerpt from 'Slavonic Dance' by Dvořák.

Read through the features below very carefully before listening to CD track 42. Try to answer part (a) after hearing the recorded excerpt no more than **twice**.

(a) Listen to CD track 42 and tick **three boxes** to identify features present in the music.

☐ Accelerando   ☐ Ascending chromatic scale

☐ Descending chromatic scale   ☐ Three against two

☐ Accents   ☐ Through-composed

☐ Diminished chord   ☐ Leitmotiv

☐ Hemiola

Listen to CD track 42 again and answer questions (b) and (c). Try to complete your answers after listening to the excerpt again no more than **twice**.

(b) Name two percussion instruments which play in the excerpt.

(i)

(ii)

(c) This piece incorporates elements from a country's traditional folk music. Name the concept which describes this practice.

Listening Exercise 40: CD Track 43

This exercise features an excerpt from a movement titled 'Aquarium' from *Carnival of the Animals* by Saint-Saëns.

Read through the features below very carefully before listening to CD track 43. Try to complete your answer after hearing the recorded excerpt no more than **three** times.

Listen to CD track 43 and tick **four boxes** to describe features present in the music.

☐ Accelerando   ☐ Hemiola

☐ Arpeggios   ☐ Sequence

☐ Staccato   ☐ Stretto

☐ Pedal   ☐ Modulation

☐ Programmatic   ☐ Glissando

Listening Exercise 41: CD Track 44

Read through the features below very carefully before listening to CD track 44. Try to answer part (a) after hearing the recorded excerpt no more than **twice**.

(a) Listen to CD track 44 and tick **three boxes** to identify features present in the music.

☐ Sequence   ☐ Impressionist

☐ Irregular metres   ☐ Imitation

☐ Three against two   ☐ Plagal cadence

☐ Added 6th chord   ☐ Dotted rhythms

☐ Tritone

Listen to CD track 44 again and answer questions (b), (c) and (d). Try to complete your answers after listening to the excerpt again no more than **twice**.

(b) From which musical period (Classical, Romantic, late Romantic) does the excerpt come?

(c) From which type of composition is the excerpt taken?

(d) Tick **one** box to describe another feature present in the music.

☐ Rubato

☐ Cymbals

☐ Col legno

☐ Through-composed

For Practice

On pages 41 and 42 there are Classical and Romantic Music Listening Charts for you to note down your observations as you listen to recordings (chosen by you or your teacher) of the various musical styles from these periods. For extra guidance, see How to Use This Book, page 6.

Classical Music Listening Chart

Title	Form/ Structure	Concepts/Features
	Symphony	
	Opera	
	Concerto	
	Sonata	

Romantic and Late Romantic Music Listening Chart

Title	Form/Structure	Concepts/Features
	Symphony	
	Opera	
	Concerto	
	Lied/Song cycle	
	Symphonic/ Tone poem	

Chapter 5

TWENTIETH-CENTURY MUSIC

Twentieth-century music refers to the various new and innovative styles/forms which began to develop after the late Romantic period (around 1910 onwards), one of the most significant being electronic music, which led to **musique concrète**.

Other innovations include **atonal** and **12-tone** music, **serialism**, **tone row**, **polytonality** and **minimalism**.

As well as art music, under the broad banner of twentieth-century music we can also include styles such as **jazz**, **jazz-funk**, **rock**, **pop** and **blues**.

Composers associated with twentieth-century music include Schoenberg, Berg, Webern, John Cage and Philip Glass.

Musical concepts associated with twentieth-century music

In this chapter, most of the musical concepts you need to know about are particularly associated with twentieth-century music, but be aware that certain concepts may also be found in music from other periods.

Before attempting exercises 42–51 make sure you fully understand the meaning of each of the Higher Music concepts below and are confident in your ability to recognise them by ear; the same applies for concepts from previous grades which also appear in the exercises. (Remember that it might help to write down a little about each concept in order to jog your memory before you begin.

- bridge
- harmonics
- inversion
- irregular metres
- jazz-funk
- microtone
- musique concrète
- polytonality
- retrograde
- serial
- time changes
- tone row
- tritone

'At a Glance' Listening Reference Chart

Style/Form/Concept	Characteristic features	Period
Jazz-funk	Fusion of jazz and funk styles. Rhythm of funk music incorporated with jazz harmony and typical rock instruments. **Improvisation** used.	Twentieth century
Serial/note row	Notes, pitches, rhythms, dynamics, etc. set into a specific order or fixed series. The twelve notes of the **chromatic** scale might be set into an order which creates a **series** or **note row**. The series can be altered with techniques such as **inversion**, **retrograde** and **retrograde inversion**. **Atonal** music.	Twentieth century
Musique concrète	Recorded music (edited recorded sounds) which is used in performance, as opposed to music which is written down for performance. **Electronic music** which is normally created in a studio or on a computer.	Twentieth century

Hints and Tips

When first introduced to twentieth-century (or 'modern') music, especially **atonal** music, many listeners find the unusual sounds, or lack of a recognisable 'tune', off-putting. Some even instantly declare that they hate it!

Before passing rash judgements on such music, it is worth remembering that the purpose of some modern styles is not just to create a 'tune.'

Think about the last suspense or horror movie you watched. If you closed your eyes and just listened to the music you might be surprised to hear that the music is quite 'tuneless', yet when you were watching the film it did its job perfectly by adding to the suspense – perhaps without your even being fully aware of the fact.

If a composer wants to create intense or powerful emotions, he/she can often do so more effectively with techniques such as **atonality**, **serialism**, **polytonality**, etc. than can ever be achieved with **tonal** music.

So, if you can listen to some of the more unusual-sounding modern music with 'ears' which are listening for the musical effect created rather than for a melody, you will give yourself the chance to have a more profound listening experience. And if you like composing music, don't underestimate the enormous potential of modern composing techniques – especially if, for example, you fancy scaring your listeners witless!

The following ten listening exercises contain multiple choice and short answer questions.

Listening Exercise 42: CD Track 45
Read through the features below very carefully before listening to CD track 42. Try to complete your answer after hearing the recorded excerpt no more **three** times.

Listen to CD track 42 and tick **four boxes** to describe features present in the music.

☐ Three against two   ☐ Concerto

☐ Pause (fermata)   ☐ Timpani roll

☐ Staccato   ☐ Crescendo

☐ Sonata   ☐ Rhythmic ostinato

☐ Tremolando/Tremolo   ☐ Col legno

Listening Exercise 43: CD Track 46
Read through the features below very carefully before listening to CD track 46. Try to answer part (a) after hearing the recorded excerpt no more than **three** times.

(a) Listen to CD track 46 and tick **four boxes** to identify features present in the music.

☐ Tone row   ☐ Snare drum

☐ Harmonics   ☐ Triangle

☐ Minimalism   ☐ Glockenspiel

☐ Whole-tone scale   ☐ Timpani

☐ Obbligato   ☐ Tremolando/Tremolo

Listen to CD track 46 again and answer questions (b), (c) and (d). Try to complete your answers after listening to the excerpt again no more than **twice**.

(b) Name the solo instrument. ⬚

(c) The Italian term (or timbre concept) which describes the smooth way in which this solo instrument plays the rapid note passages is: ⬚

(d) Tick **one** box to indicate the form of this piece.

☐ Symphony

☐ Concerto

☐ Sonata

☐ Overture

Listening Exercise 44: CD Track 47
Read through the features below very carefully before listening to CD track 47. Try to answer part (a) after hearing the recorded excerpt no more than **twice**.

(a) Listen to CD track 47 and tick **three boxes** to identify features present in the music.

☐ Microtone   ☐ Arpeggios

☐ Modulation   ☐ Mode

☐ Atonal   ☐ Cross rhythms

☐ Flutter tonguing   ☐ Staccato

☐ Glissando

HOW TO PASS HIGHER MUSIC LISTENING

Listen to CD track 47 again and answer questions (b), (c) and (d). Try to complete your answers after listening to the excerpt again no more than **twice**.

(b) Which Italian term might be used to describe the free tempo of the music?

(c) Name a musical ornament played in the piece.

(d) Tick **one** box to describe a feature present.

☐ Diminuendo

☐ Harmonics

☐ Tremolando/Tremolo

☐ Suspension

Listening Exercise 45: CD Track 48
Read through the features below very carefully before listening to CD track 48. Try to answer part (a) after hearing the recorded excerpt no more than **three** times.

(a) Listen to CD track 48 and tick **four boxes** to identify features present in the music.

☐ Tabla   ☐ Improvisation

☐ Microtone   ☐ Bending

☐ Blues scale   ☐ Musique concrète

☐ Polytonality   ☐ Retrograde

☐ Leitmotiv   ☐ Serial

Listen to CD track 48 again and answer questions (b) and (c). Try to complete your answers after listening to the excerpt again no more than **twice**.

(b) Name the solo stringed instrument.

(c) Tick **one** box to describe a feature of the music.

☐ Indonesian gamelan

☐ Ghanaian

☐ Indian

☐ Slide guitar

Listening Exercise 46: CD Track 49
Read through the features below very carefully before listening to CD track 49. Try to answer part (a) after hearing the recorded excerpt no more than **three** times.

(a) Listen to CD track 49 and tick **four boxes** to identify features present in the music.

☐ Symphony   ☐ Contrary motion

☐ Concerto   ☐ Tremolando/Tremolo strings

☐ Diminuendo   ☐ Fanfare

☐ Sequence   ☐ Triplets

☐ Accelerando   ☐ Jazz-funk

Listen to CD track 49 again and answer questions (b) and (c). Try to complete your answers after listening to the excerpt again no more than **twice**.

(b) Name the performance (or timbre) technique used by the timpani when it enters.

(c) What is the cadence heard at the end of the excerpt?

Listening Exercise 47: CD Track 50
Read through the features below very carefully before listening to CD track 50. Try to answer the question after hearing the recorded excerpt no more than **three** times.

Listen to CD track 50 and tick **four boxes** to identify features present in the music.

☐ Col legno   ☐ Stretto
☐ Neo-classical   ☐ A cappella
☐ Atonal   ☐ Sprechgesang
☐ Coloratura   ☐ Pizzicato
☐ Opera   ☐ Strophic

Listening Exercise 48: CD Track 51
Read through the features below very carefully before listening to CD track 51. Try to answer part (a) after hearing the recorded excerpt no more than **three** times.

(a) Listen to CD track 51 and tick **four boxes** to identify features present in the music.

☐ Minimalist   ☐ Polytonality
☐ Cross rhythms   ☐ Musique concrète
☐ Pedal   ☐ Harmonics
☐ Triangle   ☐ Dissonance
☐ Neo-classical   ☐ Flutter tonguing

Listen to CD track 51 again and answer questions (b) and (c). Try to complete your answers after listening to the excerpt again no more than **twice**.

(b) Name a type of drum used in the music.

(c) What is the highest pitched woodwind instrument heard in the excerpt?

Listening Exercise 49: CD Track 52
Read through the features below very carefully before listening to CD track 52. Try to answer the question after hearing the recorded excerpt no more than **three** times.

Listen to CD track 52 and tick **four boxes** to identify features present in the music.

☐ Word painting   ☐ Dissonance
☐ Melodic sequence   ☐ Bass guitar riff
☐ Middle 8   ☐ Backing vocals
☐ Minimalist   ☐ Through composed
☐ Delay   ☐ Distorted guitar

Listening Exercise 50: CD Track 53
Read through the features below very carefully before listening to CD track 53. Try to answer the question after hearing the recorded excerpt no more than **twice**.

Listen to CD track 53 and tick **three boxes** to identify features present in the music.

☐ Improvisation ☐ Riff

☐ Note row ☐ Gamelan

☐ Irregular metres ☐ Harmonics

☐ Aleatoric ☐ Whole-tone scale

☐ Ostinato

Listening Exercise 51: CD Track 54
Read through the features below very carefully before listening to CD track 54. Try to answer part (a) after hearing the recorded excerpt no more than **twice**.

(a) Listen to CD track 54 and tick **three boxes** to identify features present in the music.

☐ Polytonality ☐ Impressionist

☐ Col legno ☐ Pizzicato

☐ Trill ☐ Cross rhythms

☐ Vamp ☐ Minimalist

☐ Anacrusis

Listen to CD track 54 again and answer questions (b), (c) and (d). Try to complete your answers after listening to the excerpt again no more than **three times**.

(b) Which Italian term (or rhythm concept) describes what happens to the tempo of the music towards the end of the excerpt?

[   ]

(c) (i) Which instrument do you hear that is not normally part of the orchestra?

[   ]

(ii) Two kinds of drum are used in the music. Name **one** of these.

[   ]

(d) Tick **one** box to indicate the woodwind instrument which plays a distinctive melodic fragment during the excerpt.

☐ Flute

☐ Clarinet

☐ Oboe

☐ Bassoon

For Practice

On page 49 there is a Twentieth-century Music Listening Chart for you to note down your observations as you listen to recordings (chosen by you or your teacher) of the various musical styles from this period. For extra guidance, see How to Use This Book, page 6.

Twentieth-century Music Listening Chart

Title	Form/Structure	Concepts/Features
	Atonal	
	Jazz-funk	
	Musique concrète	
	Polytonality	
	Serialism/Note row	

MUSICAL LITERACY

In addition to knowledge of a wide range of musical concepts, the Higher Music course requires that you have a certain understanding of music notation; this is commonly referred to as music theory or musical literacy.

Part of the final Listening question paper will contain questions relating to this aspect, and you should therefore ensure that you are familiar with the rudiments of music notation.

Below is a list of the kinds of musical literacy tasks you need to be able to carry out.

On examining (at sight) the notation of a piece of music you should be able to:

◆ Re-write a short passage in treble clef at the same pitch, or one or two octaves lower, in the bass clef

◆ Describe the **interval** between two notes as a semitone, third, fifth, octave, etc.

◆ Identify **octave leaps**, **appoggiaturas**, **chords**, **cadences**, **scales**, **ornaments** and musical **symbols** (including articulation marks such as **slurs** and **accents**)

◆ Give the meaning of basic Italian terms which appear on the score

◆ Insert a missing **time signature**

◆ Identify where the main beats and up-beats are

Upon hearing the musical excerpt for which you have been given the music notation you should also be able to:

◆ Identify incorrect rhythms or notes

◆ Insert any notes or rests which are missing from a particular bar

◆ Identify where certain events occur in the music – for example, where a specific instrument starts playing. You will normally be told to do this by placing a cross **X** (or another letter) above the relevant note or bar

◆ Identify any special features relating to musical concepts you have studied (for example, the **style** or **texture** of the excerpt)

◆ Complete a bar of music which has been left blank or unfinished

There now follows eight literacy exercises which include questions which are typical of those you will encounter in your Listening question paper (question 4 of the Specimen Listening Question Paper in Chapter 7 is another). Note, however, that the supplementary questions which follow each exercise in this chapter are for extra practice only, and do not occur in Listening question papers.

Musical Literacy Exercise 1: CD Track 55

Listen to CD track 55 **once** whilst following the music printed at the top of the following page. Do not write anything during the first hearing. When you have done this, read through the question very carefully before listening to CD track 55 again and entering your answers. Try to complete your answers to questions i–vi after hearing the track no more than a further **three times** (four times in total).

First violins

(i) Re-write bars 5 and 6 (below), **one octave lower**, in the bass clef. Use the given empty bars.

(ii) Place a bracket ([_____]) over an octave leap.

(iii) Insert the rest omitted from bar 8.

(iv) Write the number of the bar in which the rhythm is incorrectly printed.

(v) Place a cross **X** above the note where you hear this fragment beginning in the bass accompaniment.

(vi) Complete bar 4.

Supplementary Questions for Musical Literacy Exercise 1

(i) Name the ornament which occurs in bar 1.

(ii) How many times is the rhythm of bar 1 repeated?

(iii) Describe (as a second, third, fourth, etc.) the most frequently occurring interval in the music.

(iv) Name the two kinds of accidental which occur in the music.

and

(v) Describe the function of the dots which appear either directly above or below some of the notes.

(vi) Compare bars 2–4 with bars 6–8 and note your observation. You might, for example, point out aspects of similarity (unity) and/or contrast.

Musical Literacy Exercise 2: CD Track 56

Listen to CD track 56 **once** whilst following the music printed below. Do not write anything during the first hearing. When you have done this, read through the question very carefully before listening to CD track 56 again and entering your answers. Try to complete your answers to questions i–vi after hearing the track no more than a further **three times** (four times in total).

(i) Re-write the opening 3 bars (below), **two octaves lower**, in the bass clef. Use the given empty bars.

(ii) Place a bracket (⌐   ⌐) over four notes which make a Turn.

(iii) State the time signature.

(iv) Put a box around a chromatic passing note.

(v) Write the numbers of the two consecutive bars where you hear this fragment in the bass accompaniment.

p

[   ]

Now compare this bass accompaniment fragment with the melody which plays over it and name the concept which describes a structural feature present.

[   ]

(vi) Complete bar 9.

Supplementary Questions for Musical Literacy Exercise 2

(i)   In which two bars does melodic sequence occur? [   ]

(ii) What type of cadence occurs in bars 8–9? [   ]

(iii) Describe the interval which occurs between the last note of bar 2 and the first note of bar 3. [   ]

(iv) Two rests are used in bar 2. What time value do they each have?

[   ]

(v) How many passing notes in the music are played staccato? [   ]

(vi) Which bar has the first example of anacrusis? [   ]

Musical Literacy Exercise 3: CD Track 57

Listen to CD track 57 **once** whilst following the music printed below. Do not write anything during the first hearing. When you have done this, read through the question very carefully before listening to CD track 57 again and entering your answers. Try to complete your answers to questions i–vi after hearing the track no more than a further **three times** (four times in total).

(i) Re-write bars 1–3 (below), **one octave lower**, in the bass clef. Use the given empty bars.

(ii) Complete bar 7.

(iii) Insert the rest omitted from bar 11.

(iv) State the time signature.

(v) Compare bars 8 and 9 with bars 10 and 11 and note your observation.

(vi) Place a bracket ( ) over two consecutive notes which form an octave leap.

Supplementary Questions for Musical Literacy Exercise 3

(i) Which musical concept best describes a feature of the rhythm?

(ii) Describe precisely the type of guitars you hear playing.

(iii) Describe the **last** chord you hear being played in the accompaniment as **major**, **minor**, **diminished** or **augmented**.

(iv) Which concept describes the manner in which this last chord is played.

(v) Name both the lowest note and the highest note in the excerpt, then describe the kind of compound interval they form (remember that a compound interval is one which is larger than an octave; for example, a G more than one octave above a C is a compound fifth interval).

Lowest note [ ]   Highest note [ ]

Interval [ ]

(vi) Name the symbol which appears above the last note and describe its function.

Musical Literacy Exercise 4: CD Track 58

Listen to CD track 58 **once** whilst following the music printed below. Do not write anything during the first hearing. When you have done this, read through the question very carefully before listening to CD track 58 again and entering your answers. Try to complete your answers to questions i–vi after hearing the track no more than a further **three times** (four times in total).

(i) What type of ornament is used in bars 3, 6 and 11?

(ii) Place a bracket ( ) over two consecutive notes in the accompaniment (left hand) which form an octave leap.

(iii) Name the rest which appears in bar 1 (left hand) and bar 13 (both hands).

(iv) State the time signature.

(v) Write the number of the bar in which the rhythm is incorrectly printed.

(vi) Complete the melody in bar 6 (right hand).

Supplementary Questions for Musical Literacy Exercise 4

(i) What is the meaning of 8va ---- written above the melody (right hand) notes?

(ii) Which concept describes a feature of the string bass accompaniment?

(iii) In which bars does contrary motion occur between melody (right hand) and accompaniment (left hand)?

(iv) What does mean (bar 1)?

(v) Put a box around two notes, played simultaneously, which are an octave apart.

(vi) Place a bracket (⌐‾‾‾‾⌐) over an octave leap which takes place in the melody (right hand).

Musical Literacy Exercise 5: CD Track 59

Listen to CD track 59 **once** whilst following the music printed below. Do not write anything during the first hearing. When you have done this, read through the question very carefully before listening to CD track 59 again and entering your answers. Try to complete your answers to questions i–vi after hearing the track no more than a further **three times** (four times in total).

(i)   Re-write bars 13–17 (below), **two octaves lower**, in the bass clef. Use the given empty bars.

(ii) Place a bracket (⌐‾‾‾‾⌐) over an appoggiatura.

(iii) Insert the rest omitted from bar 9.

(iv) Write the number of the bar in which the rhythm is incorrectly printed.

(v)   Write the numbers of the two consecutive bars where you hear this fragment played by the timpani

(vi) Complete bar 10.

Supplementary Questions for Musical Literacy Exercise 5

(i)   Which bar (or bars) contains the notes of a D major chord?

(ii) What type of cadence occurs at bars 8–9 and bars 16–17?

(iii) What does **tr** mean (bars 8 and 16)?

(iv) Describe the ornament (the two small notes) used in bars 8 and 16.

(v)   Name the concept which describes the rhythmic feature used in bar 1.

(vi) Compare bars 1–9 with bars 9–17 and comment on your observation.

Musical Literacy Exercise 6: CD Track 60

Listen to CD track 60 **once** whilst following the music printed at the top of the following page. Do not write anything during the first hearing. When you have done this, read through the question very carefully before listening to CD track 60 again and entering your answers. Try to complete your answers to questions i–vi after hearing the track no more than a further **three times** (four times in total).

(i) Re-write bars 21–24 (below), **one octave lower**, in the bass clef. Use the given empty bars.

(ii) In bars 1 and 2 the violins play two different notes simultaneously. Place a bracket over the first occurrence of two other notes (played separately) which are one octave higher than these notes. Note: you should place a bracket over each of the two notes.

(iii) Insert the rest omitted from bar 8.

(iv) Name the symbol beneath the note in bar 10.

(v) Name the ornament played by the piano in bars 11–21.

(vi) Write the bar number at which you hear this fragment begin in the string bass accompaniment.

Supplementary Questions for Musical Literacy Exercise 6

(i) What is the meaning of the word **TUTTI**?

(ii) What is the style/form of the composition from which the music is taken?

(iii) In which bar do the notes of a C major chord occur?

(iv) In how many bars does staccato occur in the violins?

(v) Which concept describes what takes place between the violins and solo piano between bars 21 and 29?

(vi) How many passing notes are there in the music of the first violins part?

Musical Literacy Exercise 7: CD Track 61

Listen to CD track 61 **once** whilst following the music printed below. Do not write anything during the first hearing. When you have done this, read through the question very carefully before listening to CD track 61 again and entering your answers. Try to complete your answers to questions i–vi after hearing the track no more than a further **three times** (four times in total).

(i) Re-write bars 3–6 (below), **one octave lower**, in the bass clef. Use the given empty bars.

MUSICAL LITERACY

(ii) Place a cross **X** above the bar in which the oboe starts playing the melody in unison with the violins.

(iii) Name the melody concept used in bars 3–4, 7–8, 11–12, and 15–16.

(iv) Compare bars 3–11 with bars 11–18 and note your observation.

(v) Two kinds of timbre (or articulation) marks are printed on the music, indicating how the violins should play certain notes. Name both of these.

and

(vi) Complete bar 12.

Supplementary Questions for Musical Literacy Exercise 7

(i)   What is the interval between the lowest and highest note in the music?

(ii) How many original bars of music are there in the excerpt – that is, bars upon which the full excerpt is based?

(iii) In the opening two bars the horns and cellos begin playing an accompaniment before the entry of the violins at bar 3. Which concept describes a feature of this accompaniment, up to bar 11?

(iv) How many musical phrases are there in the excerpt?

(v) Put a bracket over two notes which form a compound fifth interval (remember that a compound interval is one which is larger than an octave).

(vi) Explain the meaning of **𝄵** which indicates the time signature.

Musical Literacy Exercise 8: CD Track 62

Listen to CD track 62 **once** whilst following the music printed below and on the following page. Do not write anything during the first hearing. When you have done this, read through the question very carefully before listening to CD track 62 again and entering your answers. Try to complete your answers to questions i–vi after hearing the track no more than a further **three times** (four times in total).

(i) Re-write bars 1–4 of the second violins part (below), **one octave lower**, in the bass clef. Use the given empty bars.

(ii) Place a bracket over the first example of an octave leap.

(iii) Place a box around an appoggiatura.

(iv) Describe the interval between the bracketed notes at (a), (b), (c) and (d)

(a)

(b)

(c)

(d)

(v) In which bar does the oboe begin playing?

(vi) Complete bar 6.

Supplementary Questions for Musical Literacy Exercise 8

(i) Compare bars 1 and 14 and note your observations.

(ii) What type of melodic device is used in bars 7 and 8 (second violins)?

(iii) Curved lines are used in the music to indicate certain performance instructions. Explain the meaning of:

(a) the curved lines in bar 1 (violins 1 and 2)

(b) the curved lines in bars 9–13 (violin 2)

(iv) What is the meaning of **cresc.** - - - - - (bar15)?

(v) In which bar does contrary motion occur between Violins I and Violins II?

(vi) Explain the meaning of **sf** ⟩ **pp** at bars 5–6.

Chapter 7

SPECIMEN LISTENING QUESTION PAPER

Specimen Listening Paper Question 1: CD Track 63   *Marks*

The music in this question comes from a song by Curtis Mayfield.

Read through the list of features below very carefully before listening to CD track 63. Try to answer part (a) after hearing the recorded excerpt no more than **three times**.

(a) Listen to CD track 63 and tick **four** boxes to identify features present in the music.

☐ Guitar riff

☐ Backing vocals

☐ Jazz-funk

☐ 12-string guitar

☐ Middle 8

☐ Syllabic word setting

☐ Three against two

☐ Glissando

☐ Latin percussion ensemble   **4**

Listen to CD track 63 again and answer questions (b) and (c). Try to complete your answers after listening to the excerpt again no more than **twice**.

(b) Focus on the percussion instruments in this excerpt, then name the type of drums you hear playing at the beginning of (and throughout) the music.

    1

(c) Describe the style of the music (e.g. Pop, Rock, Ragtime, etc.).

    1

Total marks Question 1: (6)   ☐

Specimen Listening Paper Question 2: CD Track 64

This excerpt comes from *Introduction and Allegro* by Maurice Ravel. A 'musical map' of the excerpt is laid out below; read the question very carefully before listening to CD track 64. As you can see, you are required to insert information in the highlighted areas **1** to **4**. A voice will guide you through the excerpt as you listen. This voice will be heard immediately before the music for each of the highlighted areas is heard. Try to complete this question after listening to the excerpt no more than **three times**.

Total marks Question 2: (5)

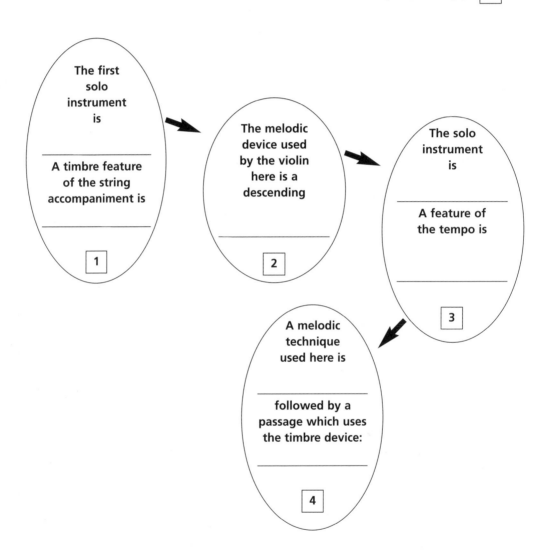

Specimen Listening Paper Question 3: CD Track 65

Read through the list of features below very carefully before listening to CD track 65. Try to answer the question after hearing the recorded excerpt no more than **twice**.

Listen to CD track 65 and tick **three boxes** to identify features present in the music.

☐ Chromatic notes

☐ Hemiola

☐ Imitation

☐ Air

☐ Mordent

☐ Pavan

☐ Renaissance

☐ Through-composed

☐ Galliard

Total marks Question 3: (3) ☐

Specimen Listening Paper Question 4: CD Track 66

Marks

This question is based on music by Jean Sibelius.

Listen to CD track 66 **once** whilst following the music printed below. Do not write anything during the first listening. When you have done this, read through the question very carefully before listening to CD track 66 again and entering your answers. Try to complete your answers after hearing the track no more than a further **three times** (four times in total).

(i)   Re-write the passage below, **two octaves lower** in the bass clef. Use the given empty bars.   *1*

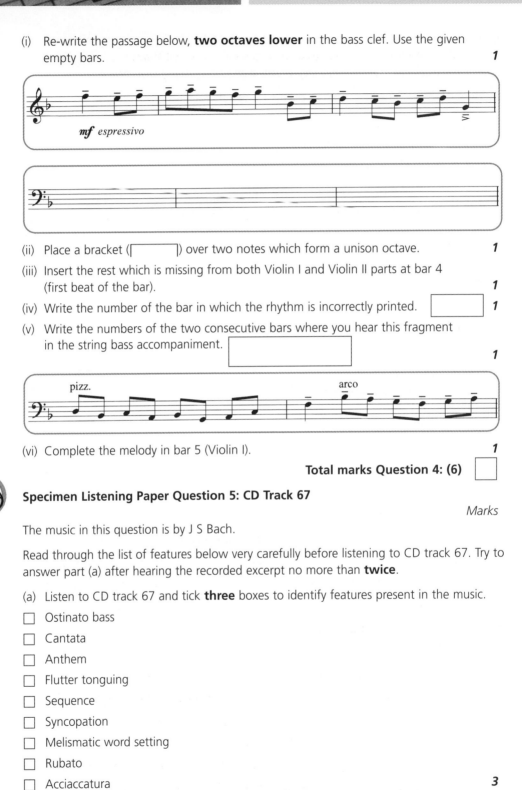

(ii) Place a bracket (☐☐☐☐) over two notes which form a unison octave.   *1*

(iii) Insert the rest which is missing from both Violin I and Violin II parts at bar 4 (first beat of the bar).   *1*

(iv) Write the number of the bar in which the rhythm is incorrectly printed. ☐   *1*

(v)   Write the numbers of the two consecutive bars where you hear this fragment in the string bass accompaniment.   *1*

(vi) Complete the melody in bar 5 (Violin I).   *1*

Total marks Question 4: (6) ☐

Specimen Listening Paper Question 5: CD Track 67

Marks

The music in this question is by J S Bach.

Read through the list of features below very carefully before listening to CD track 67. Try to answer part (a) after hearing the recorded excerpt no more than **twice**.

(a) Listen to CD track 67 and tick **three** boxes to identify features present in the music.

☐ Ostinato bass

☐ Cantata

☐ Anthem

☐ Flutter tonguing

☐ Sequence

☐ Syncopation

☐ Melismatic word setting

☐ Rubato

☐ Acciaccatura   *3*

Listen to CD track 67 again and answer questions (b), (c) and (d). Try to complete your answers after listening to the excerpt again no more than **three times**.

(b) Focus on the instrumental parts. Name the *highest pitched* woodwind instrument you hear playing a melody.

1

(c) Now focus on the bass accompaniment.

(i) Name the woodwind instrument you hear playing in the bass accompaniment.

1

(ii) Write the timbre concept which describes how most of the notes are played/articulated by this accompaniment instrument.

1

(d) Tick **one** box to describe the voice range you hear

☐ Alto

☐ Tenor

☐ Baritone

☐ Bass

1

Total marks Question 5: (7)

Specimen Listening Paper Question 6: CD Track 68
In this exercise you will describe the music you hear by inserting the correct concepts in the appropriate places in the text below.

Read through the text very carefully before listening to CD track 68. Try to complete your answers after hearing the recorded excerpt no more than **three** times.

The first woodwind instrument to be heard playing the melody is a/an _____,

and an ornament played by this instrument is a/an _____. The rising

and falling phrase structure of the melody could be described as_____and

_____ phrases. The second woodwind instrument to enter playing the

melody is a/an_____. A passage of music then follows in which both of

these woodwind instruments share the melody by alternating with each other and

also playing in _____. Another ornament heard in this section of music is

a/an _____, and a melodic device used is _____. The

Italian term which describes how the music slows down at the end of this passage

is_____. A livelier section of music then begins in which the time

signature changes to _____ time from previously being

_____ time. Although the melody changes in this new section, it is

based on that of the previous section; this technique is known as

_____. Written by Stravinsky in 1920 , this piece was

composed in the earlier style of classical music; the style or structure of this

composition would therefore be referred to as _____.

Total marks Question 6: (5)

Specimen Listening Paper Question 7: CD tracks 69 and 70

CD Tracks 69 and 70. You will now compare two excerpts of vocal music. Listed in the **left** column of the answer pages which follow are a range of musical concepts. From that column you should select features which are present in the excerpts by placing a tick in the appropriate column (**EXCERPT 1, EXCERPT 2, COMMON TO BOTH EXCERPTS**). The number of marks given at the bottom of each column in **[GRID 2] FINAL ANSWER** indicates the maximum number of concepts that should be ticked in that column.

Read the list of concepts (in column 1) carefully before listening to CD excerpt 69 and CD excerpt 70, and tick the musical concepts in each piece under the headings given in **[GRID 1]. This is your rough work.**

After listening to each excerpt no more than **three times** you should put your final answers in **[GRID 2]**.

Total marks Question 7: (8)

[GRID 1] ROUGH WORKING ONLY

CONCEPTS	EXCERPT 1 (Track 69)	EXCERPT 2 (Track 70)	COMMON TO BOTH EXCERPTS
MELODIC Trill			
Vibrato			
Atonal			
Triplets			
Microtone			
HARMONIC Interrupted cadence			
Tierce de Picardie			
Polytonality			
Pizzicato			
Cluster chords			
STRUCTURAL Inverted pedal			
Ostinato			
Cadenza			
Aria			
Polyphonic			
STYLES/FORMS Baroque			
Classical			
Romantic			
Symphony			
Concerto			

[GRID 2] FINAL ANSWER

CONCEPTS	EXCERPT 1 (Track 69)	EXCERPT 2 (Track 70)	COMMON TO BOTH EXCERPTS
MELODIC Trill			
Vibrato			
Atonal			
Triplets			
Microtone			
HARMONIC Interrupted cadence			
Tierce de Picardie			
Polytonality			
Pizzicato			
Cluster chords			
STRUCTURAL Inverted pedal			
Ostinato			
Cadenza			
Aria			
Polyphonic			
STYLES/FORMS Baroque			
Classical			
Romantic			
Symphony			
Concerto			
	2 marks	3 marks	3 marks

GLOSSARY OF MUSICAL CONCEPTS

Higher Level

Higher Melody Concepts

Acciaccatura – a note which is to be played as quickly as possible before the note it precedes. This is an *ornament*, written smaller than standard notes, with a line scored across it indicating that it has no time value and should be 'crushed in' very quickly.

Appoggiatura – a slightly discordant note on a strong beat which resolves, normally by moving one step upwards or (less often) downwards, onto the following note on the weaker beat. This is an *ornament* which is counted for *half* the value of the note it precedes and can be written either as a standard note or as a small grace note.

Harmonic minor – a version of the minor scale where the 7th note is raised by a semitone when the scale is both *ascending* and *descending*. For example, the notes of the scale of A harmonic minor are: (ascending) A B C D E F G♯ A, (descending) A G♯ F E D C B A.

Melodic minor – a version of the minor scale where the 6th and 7th notes are raised by a semitone when the scale is ascending, but lowered again by one semitone when the scale descends. For example, the notes of the scale of A melodic minor are: (ascending) A B C D E F♯ G♯ A, (descending) A G F E D C B A.

Microtone – a musical interval where the distance between two notes is less than a semitone. Microtones occur in some kinds of ethnic music and have been used since the time of ancient Greece, but it was not until the end of the nineteenth century that they appeared in Western music, when various composers began experimenting with quarter tones. Specially tuned pianos and organs were used at first (although microtones can also be produced on string instruments such as the guitar by bending the strings), but with the later development of electronic music in the twentieth century the scope for producing microtonal music greatly increased. Composers such as Bloch, Ohana and Carrilo have written this type of music.

Mode – a type of scale used in early music (Medieval and Renaissance periods) before tonal music (music with a key) was developed – although modal music is still in use today, especially in folk, rock and some ethnic music. The seven basic modes are called *Ionian, Dorian, Phrygian, Lydian, Mixolydian, Aeolean* and *Locrian*, and in their simplest form correspond to the notes C, D, E, F, G, A and B respectively. For example, if you begin on the note D on a keyboard instrument and play only the successive *white* keys for an octave, this is the *Dorian* mode. Do the same on the note F and you will play the notes of the *Lydian* mode. The specific order of tones and semitones (no black keys are used) gives each mode its unique sound.

Mordent – an *ornament* consisting of the written note followed by a rapid playing of the note a step above and then the written note again.

Tone row (or note row) – the order of the notes (selected by the composer) in a piece of twelve-note music – that is, music which uses the twelve notes (all the semitones) in an octave to create *atonal* compositions.

Tritone ('three tones') – a musical interval resulting from three whole tones. For example, the notes G–A–B–C♯ form three whole tone intervals (the notes are a tone apart); the interval between the first and last notes, G–C♯, is an augmented fourth, and is known as a tritone. Tritones are exactly half an octave.

Turn – an *ornament* consisting of four notes, indicated by the symbol ∾ above a single note. The ornament begins on (1) the note above the written note, followed by (2) the written note again, then (3) the note below, and finally (4) the written note once again. The rhythm of the turn depends on the value of the original written note, but normally involves four notes of equal time value. For example, a turn on a crotchet (quarter note) beat would be played as four semiquavers (sixteenth notes).

Higher Harmony Concepts

Added 6th chord – a chord which has the 6th note of the scale added to it – for example, the C major triad is made up of the notes C, E, G, and the sixth note of the C major scale is A, so the notes of the C6 chord are C, E, G, A. (See also *Chords and Cadences*, Chapter 1, page 9.)

Augmented chord – a chord made up of major third intervals – for example, the notes of the G augmented chord are G, B, D♯. (See also *Chords and Cadences*, Chapter 1, page 9.)

Diminished 7th chord – a diminished chord (a triad made up of minor third intervals) with a diminished 7th interval (from the root note) added on top – for example, the notes of the D diminished chord are D, F, A♭, and with the added diminished 7th interval the notes are D, F, A♭ and C♭ (D dim7). (See also *Chords and Cadences*, Chapter 1, page 9.)

Diminished chord – a chord made up of minor third intervals; for example, the notes of the D diminished chord are D, F, A♭. (See also *Chords and Cadences*, Chapter 1, page 9.)

Dominant 7th chord – the dominant chord (chord V) with a minor 7th interval added on top – for example, in the key of C major the dominant chord (chord V) is G major and the seventh note above G is F, so the dominant 7th chord in the key of C is G7 (consisting of the notes G, B, D, F). (See also *Chords and Cadences*, Chapter 1, page 9.)

Interrupted cadence – a *cadence* where chord V (the dominant chord) is followed by chord VI (the submediant chord), to create a slightly unexpected change of direction (or a little surprise) in the harmony, since the 'expected' chord I (which would complete a V–I *perfect cadence*) is replaced by chord VI (a minor chord) and so has 'interrupted' the perfect cadence. (See also *Chords and Cadences*, Chapter 1, page 9.)

Plagal cadence – a *cadence* where chord IV (the subdominant chord) is followed by chord I (the tonic chord). Sometimes called an 'Amen' cadence because it is often used at the end of hymns on the word 'Amen'. (See also *Chords and Cadences*, Chapter 1, page 9.)

Polytonality – when more than two different keys are used *at the same time* in a piece of music.

Higher Rhythm Concepts

Augmentation – where a passage of music is repeated in longer note values than when it was first played.

Diminution – where a passage of music is repeated in shorter note values than when it was first played.

Hemiola – a rhythmic effect created by articulating two bars of music in *triple metre* in such a way that they sound like three bars of music in *duple metre*, sometimes achieved by changing the time signature from 3/4 to 6/8 or vice versa. A popular device in *Renaissance* music and used in different kinds of music ever since.

Irregular metres – when the number of beats per bar in a piece of music (the time signatures) change frequently, creating an irregular beat – for example, 3/4 – 2/4 – 6/8.

Three against two – where the notes of a *triplet* play at the same time as two notes which 'add up' to the same value – for example, three crotchet triplet notes might play against two crotchet beats.

Time change – when the time signature suddenly changes in a piece of music – for example, 4/4 – 3/4.

Higher Structure/Texture/Design Concepts

Antiphonal – a term which describes music or a method of performing where an ensemble is divided into two or more smaller groups which vary between playing/singing together and alternating with each other.

Basso Continuo – a term, sometimes abbreviated to 'continuo', for the instrument or instruments responsible for establishing the harmony in a piece of (mainly) baroque music. The continuo can consist of a single instrument such as *organ* (normally used for sacred music), *harpsichord* or (for smaller ensembles) *lute*, or, where a more *contrapuntal* texture is required in the bass part, a *cello*, *bassoon* or *bass viol* (for more about *viols* see under *consort*, page 75). More than one instrument would normally be used for the continuo, especially in larger-scale works, and in a late Baroque concerto separate continuo instruments could be used for the *ripieno* and *concertino* sections of the orchestra (see entries for *ripieno* and *concertino*). As the main role of the continuo was to support the melody by providing harmony and a bass line, it was gradually replaced in the classical period when composers wrote all the required harmony notes into the music itself, but the continuo continued to play a role in certain compositions.

Bridge – a passage which links two main sections of music together. For example, in a pop song the bridge might link a verse to the chorus, and in sonata form the bridge passage is used to link themes together in the Exposition – which involves a key modulation. (See also entry for *sonata form*, page 75.)

Countersubject – see entry for *fugue*, page 77.

Episode – can mean either a secondary section in a piece of music (such as one of the contrasting episodes in a *rondo*) or any passage in a *fugue* where the *subject* (main thematic material) is not played.

Exposition – the opening section in both *sonata* and *fugue* forms (see entries for *sonata form*, page 75, and *fugue*, page 77).

Inversion – has three distinct meanings. (1) where the notes of a chord are rearranged so that the root note is replaced by another note in the chord. For example, in the chord of C major the notes are C, E, and G, with C being the lowest (root) note. If we replace the C with the next highest note, E, we create a *first inversion* of the C chord. Making the G the lowest note will result in a *second inversion* of the C chord. A form of musical 'shorthand' indicates first and second inversion chords with the letters 'b' and 'c' respectively. For example, if C major is the tonic chord (I), and its first inversion is used, this would be represented as Ib, and the second inversion as Ic. So, a *second inversion* of the *dominant* chord (which in the key of C major is *G major*) would be written as Vc. (2) The term *inversion* also applies to the technique of repeating a passage of music as a mirror image of itself, resulting in the repeating passage moving in opposite directions (or contrary motion) to the first. (3) The word *inversion* is also used to describe the inversion of an interval. For example, the interval between C and E is a *third*, but when this is inverted (E to C) it becomes a *sixth*.

Leitmotiv – a musical idea or theme which represents a particular thing, person or idea in a piece of music. The leitmotiv will return periodically at relevant points in the piece, perhaps to remind us subtly of the person/thing on which the leitmotiv is based. The device is mainly associated with the Romantic period (although it appeared much earlier) and dramatic works such as opera – for example, *Tristan und Isolde* and *Das Rheingold* by Richard Wagner.

Real Answer – see entry for *fugue*, page 77.

Retrograde – where a passage of notes is played backwards. The technique was first used in Medieval and Renaissance music, but is also important in 12-note (or *note row*) music such as Schoenberg's where 12-note rows can be used in both *retrograde* and *retrograde inversion* (see entry for *inversion*, page 74).

Ritornello – a term used mainly in Baroque music to describe a passage which keeps recurring (normally alternating with the soloist), mainly in the instrumental *tutti* ('everyone') sections of a baroque *concerto* or *aria*.

Sonata Form – the most important structure for instrumental music from the Classical period to the twentieth century. The form consists of three main sections: (1) the first section, the *exposition*, 'exposes' the main musical material, which consists of a number of *themes* divided into the *first subject* (in the *tonic* key) and the *second subject* (normally in either the *dominant* or *relative major* key), which are separated by a *transition* or *bridge* passage, and concluded by a *codetta* (brief *Coda*). (2) the second section, the *development*, 'develops' the material of the *exposition* by *repeating* it with *variation* and in several different keys, ending in the *tonic* key in preparation for the next section. (3) the final section, the *recapitulation*, 'recaps' the themes used in the *exposition* (perhaps with some key changes), normally in the same order, but with the *second subject* now in the *tonic* key. Sometimes an *Introduction* and a *Coda* are added to this basic sonata structure.

Stretto – the term can mean either (1) the technique of introducing (in quick succession) two or more entries of the *subject* (main theme) in a *fugue*, or (2) a change to a faster *tempo* in a climactic or dramatic point in a piece of music – such as the finale of an opera.

Subject – see entry for *fugue*, page 77.

Tonal answer – see entry for *fugue*, page 77.

Transition – a passage, often involving modulation, which leads one main section of a piece of music into another (such as the *bridge passage* joining the first and second subjects together in sonata form).

Higher Timbre Concepts

Coloratura – a term used, especially in vocal music, to describe sections decorated with florid, elaborate passages of notes or ornamentation. The technique requires considerable skill of the singer (normally a soprano); good examples can be found in some of Mozart's operas.

Concertino – The solo group in a Baroque concerto or 'concerto grosso'. Later, the term could also mean a small-scale concerto.

Consort – an old English term (which is derived from the Italian word 'concerto') for a small group of musicians. It is used mainly in reference to sixteenth and seventeenth century music. The term can apply to groups of voices (with or without instruments), instrumental groups, and sometimes even to the music itself, but usually meant groups who played different kinds of musical instruments such as flute, lute, treble and bass viol, bandora and cittern. (*Viols* were bowed string instruments of varying sizes with frets; smaller versions such as the treble viol (resembling a violin) would be played vertically on the lap, while the larger bass viol was played, like a cello, between the performer's legs. The *bandora* was a plucked string bass instrument with six or seven metal strings. The *cittern* was a wire string instrument which was plucked using a plectrum.) Composers of consort music include Purcell, Byrd and Morley.

Harmonics – the individual sounds which are usually part of a musical note, and which give it its particular tone quality. Different instruments produce different numbers and types of harmonics, even when playing the same note, and this contributes to an instrument's unique sound. Individual harmonics can be produced on many instruments; these are 'extra' high-pitched notes of a particular sound quality, with a clarity and sustain that cannot be achieved in normal playing. These kinds of harmonics can be produced on wind instruments by altering lip pressure and (in the case of woodwind instruments) by opening a nodal hole in the instrument; string instruments can produce 'natural' harmonics by touching a string at specific points (frets in the case of a guitar) before playing the string, and 'artificial' harmonics by holding down a note (as in normal playing) and touching the string either a fourth or an octave higher (depending on the instrument).

Ripieno – the *tutti* ('everyone') or *concerto grosso*, as distinct from the solo group (or 'concertino') of a Baroque orchestra, especially in concertos.

Sprechgesang – 'speech song': a vocal technique which is half way between singing and speech; used by twentieth-century composers including Schoenberg and Berg.

Higher Style/Form Concepts

Air – a simple (often fairly slow) melody for voice or an instrument, but from about 1571 the term could also apply to lute music and ensemble songs; composers of this style include court lutenist John Dowland. The term 'air' was also used in late Baroque suites and for instrumental pieces by Purcell, and by the mid-seventeenth century in England it described a type of simple song. In traditional Scottish music an air is a slow tune that is either sung or played on an instrument such as the bagpipes or fiddle.

Anthem – a short choral work, whose text is taken from a moral or religious text in English, normally intended for performance in Church of England religious services. Early anthems (around 1550) consisted of four *contrapuntal* vocal parts which *imitated* each other, sometimes with *soloists* and organ *accompaniment*. In 1600 a development was the *verse style* or *verse anthem* (examples of which were written by English composers Byrd and Morley), where verses for solo voices and instrumental accompaniment (usually organ) alternated with choral passages. After 1661 a new style evolved with a *homophonic* texture and a succession of contrasting verses with occasional choruses. Purcell contributed to the development of this style, as well as to the *full anthem* and the newer *orchestral anthem*. Anthem composing continued in the eighteenth century with composers including Handel, and led to the development of the *American anthem*. The nineteenth century saw the Victorian revival of anthem composing, and the style even influenced twentieth-century composers such as Britten, Walton, and Vaughan Williams to write anthem-like pieces.

Ballett – a type of vocal concert piece, popular in England and Italy around 1600, similar to the *madrigal* but more dance-like with a *fa-la* refrain (or chorus) in the English version.

Chaconne/Passacaglia – although beginning as two distinct forms, in the art music of the Baroque period there is little or no noticeable difference between the chaconne and the passacaglia: both are dances based on *variation* form, often associated with the use of a *ground bass*. Composers who wrote these works include Monteverdi, Lully, Bach and Purcell.

Chant – dating from as far back as the fourth century, the chant began as a form of slow singing used in religious and pagan ceremonies, long before any musical notation system had been devised. It developed and diversified over the centuries, and by medieval times 'plainchant' or 'plainsong' (a *monophonic unison* chant in Latin) was used in the Christian church. From this came the 'Gregorian chant', used in the Roman Catholic mass, consisting of a single vocal line with a free rhythm which followed the syllables of the Latin text – and therefore often had an irregular *metre* (by this stage chants were being written down using an early system which was quite unlike modern notation). This type of chant had three styles: *syllabic* (where each syllable is sung to a single, separate note), *neumatic* (where between two and twelve notes accompany a single syllable), and *melismatic* (where single syllables might be sung to many notes). Later, the *Anglican chant*, a harmonised religious melody used for psalm-singing, was used in the Church of England.

Chorale prelude – see entry for *chorale*, page 95.

Concerto grosso – a kind of Baroque concerto comprising a *concertino* (small group of instruments or soloists) and the *ripieno* or *concerto grosso* (main group of instruments). The purpose of having two groups was mainly so that they could provide contrast with each other.

Da capo aria – an aria in *ternary form* (ABA) where the instruction '*Da Capo*' (go back to the beginning) is given at the end of the B section, as opposed to the A section being written out again.

Fugue – a musical form, usually instrumental and in three or four parts, where each part (or 'voice' as they are often called) imitates the other successively, creating a *contrapuntal* texture. The main opening theme in a fugue (called the *subject*) is first played in the tonic key, and this is then imitated by another part (called the *answer*) normally in the dominant key. This alternating pattern is repeated throughout the fugue at different *octaves*. (A 'real' answer is one which is a precise note-for-note *transposition* of the *subject*, but sometimes this isn't desirable – where a 'real' answer would create *dissonance* with another part, for example – and certain intervals are altered to fit with the rest of the music. This is known as a 'tonal' answer.) When the *answer* is being played, the first voice will play a new main theme called the *countersubject* which is also followed by an *answer*. In between this overlapping texture of subject and answer phrases are sections of music called *episodes*, but the pattern doesn't have to be so strict, and although this is the basic formula, many composers (notably J S Bach) varied the plan by adding original touches and variations to the general structure.

Galliard – A lively instrumental court dance (although it became a slower piece in its later style) in *triple metre* (three beats per bar), dating back to at least the fifteenth century. Normally played after a *pavan* to which it is thematically related, the galliard often uses a simple *homophonic* style (with the main tune in the upper part) and *hemiola*. Famous examples of the galliard can be found in the lute music of English composers John Dowland and Robert Johnson.

Jazz-funk – a fusion of jazz and funk music which appeared around the mid 1970s. Artists in the genre include James Taylor (the James Taylor Quartet), Roy Ayers and Stanley Clarke.

Late Romantic – the last of the three periods of the Romantic era, lasting from about 1890 to around 1910. The Romantic era existed from approximately 1790 to 1910, the early period ending around 1850 and the middle period 1890. Late Romantic composers include Mahler, Rachmaninov and R Strauss.

Lied (plural: *Lieder*) – German word for a song, but it refers more particularly to an art song of the Romantic era written by composers such as Schumann, Mendelssohn, Wagner and R Strauss. Despite this association with Romantic music, the term *Lied* has been used since the fifteenth century, but Classical composers (including Mozart and Beethoven) began to develop the style, and this practice was continued by Romantic composers. The songs (*Lieder*) – which were often *strophic* or *ternary* in structure, and *accompanied* by piano – focused on poetry, drama, scene-setting and character in an expressive way that was typical of the Romantic period. The piano accompaniment became more important as the Romantic era progressed, and composers such as Brahms, Wolf, Liszt and Schubert (who was widely recognised as one of the finest lieder composers) wrote intricate piano music for their lieder. The development of lieder continued into the twentieth century, even though the tradition of song with piano accompaniment was lessening, and Mahler (who also wrote lieder with orchestral accompaniment), Schoenberg and Berg all composed original lieder.

Madrigal – a contrapuntal piece for several voices, sometimes with independent instrumental accompaniment, which developed from the *motet* and the French *chanson*. The word *madrigal* was first used in the fourteenth century to refer to poetic as well as musical forms, but from about the mid-sixteenth century a madrigal was typically a musical work based on a non-religious verse (although some sacred madrigals were written) which concerned love or other human emotions. Madrigals for three voices and instrumental accompaniment were popular, and in the late sixteenth century composers experimented with *word painting*, *chromaticism* and *rhythmic* and *harmonic contrast*. One such composer was Monteverdi, who introduced a continuo part to the madrigal, and whose bold musical inventiveness in general helped to pave the way for the innovations of the proceeding Baroque period. Although beginning in Italy, the madrigal later became popular in England, and by the first part of the seventeenth century solo madrigals were also being composed.

Mass – a large-scale vocal work based mainly on the Roman Catholic High Mass (which was sung). The mass is divided into two parts: the *Ordinary*, which is the unchanging sections of the mass (the *Kyrie, Gloria, Credo, Sanctus Benedictus, Agnus Dei* and *Benedicamus Domino*), and the *Proper*, a musical setting (normally based on plainsong) of those parts of the mass which were varied depending on the occasion (the *Introit, Gradual, Alleluia, Offertory* and *Communion*). Dating from the seventh century, the mass underwent various transformations over the centuries which were partly influenced by musical developments. The *chants* used in the earliest masses became the melodic material for the early *organum* of the tenth century, and from this the use of *polyphony* entered the mass. By the mid-fifteenth century the *cantus firmus* or *tenor* mass was firmly established, which often used melodies from non-religious *chansons* as a source for the tenor part around which original melodies were composed. This practice of weaving existing material with new music was common, and masses could be based on *chansons*, *motets* or *madrigals* written by late Renaissance composers such as Palestrina and Morales. There were also *freely invented* masses, *canonic masses* and *paraphrase masses*, all of which used different kinds of musical techniques in their composition. Masses which used either choruses with instrumental doubling, or solo voices and independent instrumental accompaniment, influenced the development of the *cantata mass* which divided the various sections of the mass into several movements; this style was used by Baroque composers, including J S Bach, whose B minor Mass is the finest example. Haydn and Mozart's masses of the Classical period show the influence of the symphony in their style, and later masses by Beethoven (the *Missa Solemnis* and the Mass in C), Liszt, Bruckner and Stravinsky were written for concerts or special occasions rather than religious services.

Motet – a *polyphonic* vocal composition, often with two vocal parts and two instrumental parts, mainly religious (although non-religious motets exist), which was important from Medieval times through to the eighteenth century and also influenced the development of other musical forms. Earlier motets were built upon an existing religious tenor voice part, the *cantus firmus*, over which up to three upper voices sang a faster melody; this style became popular around 1450, by which time it was common for motets to consist of between four and six individual parts. *Imitative counterpoint* and *polyphony* were used in the sixteenth century motet, and the Baroque period saw the inclusion of instrumental parts doubling the voices as well as a continuo accompaniment. Voices with continuo (the '*vocal concerto*') became very popular, and by the mid-Baroque period the *orchestral motet* had developed, which was similar to the operatic forms of the time. The influence of the motet led to the appearance of the *aria*, the *chorale,* the eighteenth century *church cantata* and the *choral motet*, which was developed for weddings, funerals and special occasions – J S Bach's six motets are the finest examples of this form. Other motet composers include Palestrina, Mozart, Liszt and Brahms.

Musique concrète – a term first used in the late 1940s by electronic music composers in Paris to describe music assembled on tape from pre-recorded sounds, instead of being written down as musical notation for later live performance.

Nationalist – a term applied to music which in some way reflects aspects of the nationality of a country; this could be achieved through the use of folk melodies, traditional dance rhythms, and even the musical instruments associated with a particular country. Although composers of the seventeenth and eighteenth centuries sometimes used the folk melodies of their countries in their compositions, it wasn't until the mid-nineteenth century that Nationalism became a popular movement in music. Composers including Debussy (France), Sibelius (Finland), Holst (England), Musorgsky (Russia) and Wagner (Germany) all incorporated nationalist elements in some of their works.

Neo-classical – a term describing a twentieth-century style in which some composers (especially in the period between the two world wars) wrote music in the earlier style of classical music; examples include Stravinsky, Schoenberg and Prokofiev.

Overture – an 'introduction': a piece of orchestral music which introduces a big work, especially an opera, and may contain musical features (such as small fragments of tunes) which later appear in the main work.

Pavan – A slow and stately instrumental court dance (dating from at least the sixteenth century), normally in *duple metre* (two beats per bar), which is followed by a faster dance (or dances) in *triple metre*, particularly the *galliard*. A famous example from the Romantic era is the *Pavan pour une Infante défunte* (Pavan for a dead Infanta – a Spanish princess) by Ravel. Pavan composers include Purcell, Dowland and Byrd.

Plainchant or 'Plainsong' – a religious *monophonic unison* chant sung in Latin, which dates back to the early Christian church. Sometimes also referred to as 'Gregorian chant'. (See also entry for *chant*, page 77.)

Renaissance – a term, meaning 'rebirth' (of ancient Greek and Roman values), given to the period between the Medieval and Baroque periods (about 1430 to 1600). Music of the Renaissance includes *chansons, masses, motets* and *madrigals*, as well as instrumental *consort* music. A characteristic style of the period is *imitative counterpoint* (or *imitative polyphony*) in four or more parts, in compositions written by composers such as Palestrina and Byrd. Two very popular instruments of the time were the recorder and the lute.

Serial – a composing method where musical elements (note pitches, dynamics, etc.) are set into an order or a fixed 'series'. This normally involves setting the notes and pitches in a specific way, such as arranging the twelve notes of the *chromatic scale* into a particular order to create a series or 'row' on which an entire piece of music will be structured. This note-row or series can be altered using techniques such as *retrograde, inversion, retrograde inversion*, and by transposing the series up or down by any interval. Notes may be repeated (but the order of the notes in the series is not normally altered) and chords can also be used. Serialism began with Schoenberg in the 1920s and was adopted by his pupils Webern and Berg and later (after 1945) by Boulez, Stockhausen and Stravinsky, who expanded and developed the technique by setting elements such as note duration, attack (accents, sforzando, etc.) and dynamics into a fixed series.

Sonata – an instrumental composition with three main sections which are called the *exposition, development* and *recapitulation* (see entry for *sonata form* on page 75).

Song cycle – a group of songs where each song is complete in itself, but linked together by a common aspect such as a narrative (story) or theme. Song cycles, which evolved in the nineteenth century, were written by composers including Debussy, Schubert, Fauré, Schumann and Mahler.

Suite – a collection of pieces intended to be played in succession in a single performance to form a large instrumental work. The individual pieces were commonly a collection of dances in the same key but with a different *style/character, tempo* and *metre*. In the Baroque period the common dances were the French *Bourée* (a lively dance in duple metre), *Allemande* (a moderate-tempo dance normally in *quadruple metre*), *Courante* (a moderate-tempo dance, usually in *triple metre*, with a contrapuntal texture), *Sarabande* (a slow dance normally in *triple metre*), *Minuet* (a dance in moderate *triple metre*) and *Gigue* (a lively dance in moderate or fast tempo and usually in 3/4, 6/8 or 9/8 time). The popularity of suites faded in the classical period when other instrumental forms such as the *symphony*, *sonata* and *concerto* developed, but Mozart and later composers including Ravel, Strauss, Debussy and Schoenberg all wrote suites. The term 'suite' in the nineteenth and twentieth centuries was also used for a collection of movements from a large-scale work such as an opera or ballet, and for a group of pieces or movements linked by a single theme (a nationalist theme, for example) or a descriptive programme, such as *The Planets* by Holst.

Symphonic/Tone poem – a form of orchestral music based specifically on a story, programme, poem or event which the music alone portrays or 'narrates'. The form can be seen to have begun evolving in certain of Beethoven's overtures (the *Egmont Overture* for example) which describe actual events, and in those of Mendelssohn and Berlioz. Composers of the symphonic poem include Liszt (who introduced the term), Tchaikovsky (*Romeo and Juliet*), Saint-Saëns (*Danse macabre*), Richard Strauss (*Also sprach Zarathustra*) and Sibelius (*The Swan of Tuonela*). Nationalistic ideas were also used often in the symphonic poems of Smetana, Dvořák, Musorgsky and Borodin. The main difference between a symphony and a symphonic poem is that a symphonic poem portrays something non-musical, such as a piece of literature.

Concepts from Earlier Levels

Access 3 (equivalent to Foundation Level at Standard Grade)

Access 3 Melody Concepts

Answer – a small phrase of music (e.g. as short as two bars) which sounds as if it is 'answering' the previous phrase (the 'Question').

Ascending melody – a tune which becomes higher in pitch as it progresses.

Broken chord – when the notes of a chord are played separately rather than together.

Descending melody – a tune which becomes lower in pitch as it progresses.

Leaping melody – a tune which progresses in big jumps.

Phrase – a musical 'statement', similar in principle to a spoken phrase where the speaker would pause or take a breath before continuing with the next piece of information (the next phrase).

Question – a small phrase of music (as short as two bars) which needs to be completed with an 'Answer' phrase.

Repetition – a bar, phrase or complete section which is repeated in a piece of music.

Sequence – a passage of music which repeats at a higher or lower pitch.

Stepwise melody – a tune which progresses in small steps rather than big jumps.

Access 3 Harmony Concepts

Chord – the sounding of two or more notes at the same time; a tonic triad chord is made up of the first, third and fifth notes of a scale (e.g. the notes C, E and G make up a C chord).

Chord change – the ability to recognise (with your ear) when a chord has changed in a piece of music.

Discord/dissonance – notes or chords which create a brief out-of-tune effect in a piece of music.

Access 3 Rhythm Concepts

Accent – a musical symbol > written above or below notes or chords which are to be played slightly louder.

Accented – a musical note, phrase, chord or passage which contains accents.

Beat/Pulse – the steady main pulse in a piece of music.

Drum fill – a short flourish played on drums whose function is to link two passages together (i.e. phrases or verses) by 'filling' the gap in between these sections.

Faster, Slower – where sections of music speed up or slow down. If this is done gradually in a piece of music the term *accelerando* (or *accel.* – meaning to accelerate to a faster tempo) is used to indicate an increase in speed, and *ritardando* or *ritenuto* (or *rit.*) are used to indicate a decrease in speed. When the music changes to a faster or slower speed at the beginning of a new section, the new tempo is indicated at the start of that section (either as a precise metronome speed or with an Italian term such as *allegro*, *andante*, *moderato*, etc.).

Off the beat – where the stress or accent is off the beat (on the 'up-beat', for example – as in syncopation).

On the beat – where the stress or accent is on the main beat(s).

Pattern – a group of musical notes whose 'shape' forms a visible pattern (e.g. arpeggios); such patterns are often repeated either directly or as a sequence.

Pause (fermata) – a musical symbol 𝄐 written over a note, chord or rest to indicate that the player(s) should pause at that point.

Repetition – a passage or section of music which is repeated.

Scotch snap – a rhythm where a short note on the beat is followed by a longer one ♪ ♩. ; often used in Scottish music.

Simple time (2, 3 and 4 beats in the bar) – a time signature where the main beats are divisible by two, e.g. crotchets and minims (2/4, 3/4, 4/4, 2/2 time); opposite to compound time.

Access 3 Structure/Texture/Design Concepts

Accompanied – where the most important melody or solo in a piece of music has another instrument or instruments playing along with it (e.g. a song with piano accompaniment).

Contrast – when the music changes key, speed, mood, volume, etc.

Ensemble – two or more musicians playing together as a group.

Harmony – where notes are combined/played at the same time to produce satisfactory sounds and create texture in a piece of music.

Ostinato – the constant repetition of the same musical phrase, rhythm pattern or chords.

Repetition – where a bar, phrase or complete section is repeated in a piece of music.

Riff – a short musical phrase of around 2–4 bars long which is repeated regularly throughout a piece of music (especially in jazz, rock and pop music).

Round – a musical form where the melody is repeated in other parts at staggered intervals to create an overlapping texture (as in the children's song 'Row, row, row your boat').

Section – can mean a particular part of a piece of music (for example, the middle section) or a group within the orchestra (for example, the string section).

Single line – where only a single line of music appears – i.e. one which is not harmonised; for example, an unaccompanied melody.

Solo – a section of music or a whole piece performed by just one musician.

Unaccompanied – where no other instruments play along with the main melody or instrument in a piece of music – opposite to accompanied.

Unison/Octave – where all parts in a piece of music sing or play the same notes – either at the same pitch or an octave apart.

Access 3 Timbre Concepts

Accordion – a small reed organ comprising bellows (which, operated by the player's arm, pump air into the instrument), a treble keyboard and a bass keyboard. The bass keyboard, played with the left hand, is made up of buttons, whereas the treble keyboard, played with the right hand, may be either buttons or, more commonly, piano keys. The player 'wears' the instrument by means of shoulder straps.

Backing vocals – the singers who accompany the lead vocalist.

Blowing – the method of producing sound on any wind instrument (e.g. flute, trumpet, recorder) by using the breath.

Bowing – the method of producing sound on a string instrument (violin, cello, double bass etc.) by drawing a bow over the strings.

Brass band – a band in which different kinds of brass instruments such as trumpet, cornet, horn and euphonium are played.

Drum kit – a set of drums used in various kinds of music groups, and especially in pop, folk, rock and jazz bands. The kit can vary depending on the style of the music, but normally includes a bass drum, snare drum and at least one suspended cymbal as standard.

Fiddle – the word used for a violin when it is used to play certain kinds of music, especially folk music and traditional Scottish music.

Folk group – a band of musicians who play folk music; in Scottish folk music such a group would play instruments such as fiddle, penny whistle, accordion and guitar.

Guitars (acoustic and electric) – standard acoustic and electric guitars have six strings which are either plucked or strummed. Bass guitars (including fretless bass guitars) have four strings. Acoustic guitars include the *classical guitar* (which has nylon and wire-wound nylon strings), the *acoustic guitar* (which has steel strings), the *acoustic bass* guitar (which can have either steel or nylon strings depending on the model), the *slide guitar* (which has steel strings), and the *12-string guitar* (which has six pairs of steel strings). Electric guitars have steel strings and are plugged into an amplifier, but so-called semi-acoustic guitars of all varieties can be played either with or without amplification.

Jazz group – a band of musicians who play jazz music. Such groups can vary a lot as there are many different styles of jazz music, and may include one or more lead singers (perhaps with backing vocals also) with any combination of instruments such as piano, trumpet, trombone, saxophone, double bass, guitar, bass guitar, banjo, drums, vibraphone and xylophone.

Keyboards (acoustic and electronic) – piano, organ and synthesizer.

Lead vocals – the person who sings the main melody of a song.

Legato – smooth notes or chords with no silences in between (the opposite of staccato).

Louder, Softer – where the volume in a piece of music alters to become either louder or quieter (known as musical *dynamics*).

Orchestra – a large group of musicians who play a selection of instruments grouped into four main 'families': *woodwind* (piccolo, flute, oboe, clarinet, bassoon), *brass* (trumpet, trombone, French horn, tuba), *percussion* (timpani, woodblock, glockenspiel, gong, etc.) and *strings* (first and second violins, viola, cello, double bass). Music can be either written especially for orchestra (e.g. a symphony) or arranged for it, but in all cases the orchestra is led by a conductor who dictates the speed, dynamics and overall interpretation of a piece, and generally makes sure everyone plays well together.

Organ – although technically a wind instrument because air produces the sound through large pipes (unless it is a much smaller electric organ), an organ has a keyboard as well as foot pedals and stops (buttons which alter the volume and the type of sound produced).

Pipe band – a Scottish marching band where only bagpipes and drums are played.

Pipes – an abbreviation of 'bagpipes' or 'Uillean pipes' (which are also sometimes referred to as 'Irish pipes'. These are played in a seated position and, unlike the bagpipes, do not require air to be blown into a mouthpiece; instead air is pumped into the instrument by bellows which are operated by the player's arm).

Plucking – a method of producing sound on any string instrument by striking the strings with the fingers or (on guitars and banjo) a plectrum (a small triangular shaped object held by the fingers).

Pop group – a band of musicians who play pop music, normally using a singer (or singers), electric and bass guitars, drums and possibly keyboard.

Rock band – a band who play rock music, normally on electric and bass guitars, drums, vocals and possibly keyboard.

Scottish Dance band – a group, consisting of piano, accordion, fiddle and drums, who play traditional Scottish music.

Silence – the absence of sound; indicated on written music by *rests.*

Slapping – a technique used on string instruments such as guitar and (especially) bass guitar where the strings are slapped to produce a particular sound.

Sound – any noise which can be detected by the ears as it travels on the airwaves which surround us. Music is a collection of various 'noises' produced by musicians in order to create particular sounds and pitches.

Staccato – short, detached notes or chords.

Steel band – a group of musicians who play tuned percussion instruments which are made from oil drums. These bands began in the 1930s in the West Indies.

Striking – when an instrument is hit (with the hand, or a beater such as a drum stick) to produce a sound.

Strumming – a method of producing sound on string instruments such as guitar or banjo by quickly drawing the fingers or a plectrum (a small triangular shaped object) across the strings.

Sustained – sound which continues in a steady, unbroken flow.

Vocal/Choral – music where voice is the main instrument. Choral music involves a choir (a large group of singers) which can be made up of male voices only, female voices only, male and female voices, or children's voices (youth choir).

Voice – the creation of musical notes using the voice, as in songs.

Wind/Military band – a band of woodwind, brass and percussion musicians who often play brisk military music including marches (such as those by John Philip Sousa).

Access 3 Style/Form Concepts

Baroque – a term used to describe music from about 1600–1750 which is characterised by features such as contrast (e.g. contrasting dynamics, tempo, etc.), walking bass and ornaments. Famous Baroque composers include J S Bach, Handel and Vivaldi.

Jazz – an improvised style of music developed by African-Americans in the early twentieth century which often uses lively swing rhythms and bent pitches (discordant notes used to 'colour' the music).

Latin-American – a style which blends different kinds of music from several cultures, including Spain, the Caribbean and South America; one of its most popular versions is lively South American jazz.

March – a musical composition in *duple metre* (2 main beats per bar) intended to be marched to.

Pop – a style of music which uses modern sounds and song lyrics (words) that are normally popular with the mass public, particularly the younger generation.

Reel – a lively Scottish dance in *duple metre* (2 beats per bar) which moves in fast, smooth quavers. Also common in Ireland and North America.

Rock – a popular modern style of music which developed from Rock 'n' Roll. Rock music often uses 'heavier' lyrics and more driving beats than pop music even though both styles use electric instruments, drums and amplified singing.

Scottish – music linked closely with Scotland and traditional (early) Scottish styles such as the reel, jig, strathspey, mouth music, bothy ballad, etc.

Strathspey – a traditional Scottish dance reel in 4/4 time with a moderate tempo and characterised by a dotted rhythm – e.g. ♪. ♪ OR ♩. ♪

Waltz – a moderate tempo dance in *triple metre* (3 beats per bar).

Intermediate 1 (equivalent to General Level at Standard Grade)

Intermediate 1 Melody Concepts

Chromatic scale – a scale which moves only in semitones (e.g. C C$^\sharp$ D D$^\sharp$ E F F$^\sharp$ G G$^\sharp$ A A$^\sharp$ B C).

Imitation – when a musical phrase in one part is copied (imitated) in another part.

Major scale – a scale whose order of tones and semitones makes a pleasant or 'happy' sound (C D E F G A B C) – from this we also get major chords and major intervals.

Minor scale – a scale whose order of tones and semitones makes a serious or 'sad' sound (C D E$^\flat$ F G A$^\flat$ B$^\flat$ C) – from this we also get minor chords and minor intervals.

Ornament – extra 'decorative' notes added to a melody.

Pentatonic scale – a scale which uses only five different notes (and no semitones) to make a particular sound (e.g. C E$^\flat$ F G B$^\flat$). Used in rock, jazz, blues and folk music.

Scale – a rising or falling succession of adjacent notes.

Scat singing – a style of jazz singing where meaningless words or syllables are sung to improvised music.

Semitone – the musical interval (the distance between two notes) of half a tone. This is the smallest distance between two notes in tonal music; every consecutive note on the piano keyboard is a semitone apart.

Theme – the main tune in a piece of music.

Tone – a musical interval made up of two semitones.

Variation – when a melody or a whole section of music is changed in some way when it is repeated.

Intermediate 1 Harmony Concepts

Change of key – when a piece of music changes from one key to another (known as modulation).

Chord Progressions/changes – chord changes, e.g. between chords I, IV and V in major keys.

Drone – a constantly sustained note (normally a bass note), over which the main melody is played; bagpipes use at least one drone.

Tonality – the key of a piece of music (e.g. whether it is *major* or *minor*).

Vamp – improvising a simple chord accompaniment (normally on the piano) to a solo.

Intermediate 1 Rhythm Concepts

Anacrusis – the upbeat note (or notes) which comes before the first strong beat of a bar.

Compound time – a time signature where the main beats are divisible by three, e.g. dotted quavers (6/8, 9/8, 12/8 time).

Down beat – the strong beat at the beginning of a bar.

Speed change or tempo variations – speeding up or slowing down from the original speed; indicated by, for example, *accelerando, rallentando, ritenuto, ritardando* or *rubato*.

Syncopation – where the accent is off the main beat and on a weaker beat (the upbeat, for example).

Upbeat – the weaker beat which comes before the strong downbeat.

Intermediate 1 Structure Concepts

Arpeggio – a 'broken chord' where the notes of the chord are played one after the other (often in a rhythmic pattern) instead of all together.

Binary form – a musical structure, common in Baroque music, made up of two main sections, A and B, each of which is usually repeated. The B section is normally longer than the A section.

Canon – a musical form where the first melody is imitated by another part (or parts) before the first melody is finished – this creates a texture where tunes overlap each other in a harmonious way.

Chord – the sounding of two or more notes at the same time; a tonic triad chord is made up of the first, third and fifth notes of a scale (e.g. the notes C, E and G make up a C chord).

Contrary motion – notes or passages of music moving in opposite directions (up or down).

Descant – a decorative extra part sung above a melody. It can also refer to an instrument tuned to a particular pitch (e.g. descant recorder).

Middle 8 – a short instrumental section in a song lasting for 8 bars which links the verse with the chorus.

Minuet and trio – a musical form based on ternary structure (ABA) where the A section is the minuet and the B section the trio (a contrasting middle section, usually involving a key change).

Note cluster – a bunch of adjacent notes played together (usually applies to piano music).

Programme music – music which describes a particular scene, emotion or story (e.g. a stormy sea, rainfall, a biblical story, a person's death, etc.).

Rondo – a musical structure where the main theme (the A section) alternates with several new or contrasting sections of music known as episodes (e.g. A B A C A D A).

Ternary form – a musical structure made up of three main sections, A B A, where the B section normally provides some musical contrast and the second A section can either be an exact or altered repeat of the first A section. Sometimes the structure is A A B A.

Theme and variations – a musical form where a theme is played and then followed by a set of variations based on that theme. The variations normally include changes to the speed, key, rhythm, etc. of the main theme.

Walking bass – a bass line where the note values and speed remain constant, as though walking steadily; a common technique in Baroque music but also used in jazz and boogie-woogie.

Intermediate 1 Timbre Concepts

Ceilidh band – a group of musicians, typically consisting of a fiddler, drummer, pianist, accordionist and guitarist who play traditional Scottish Ceilidh music.

Chamber music – music for a smaller ensemble (about 3–8 players) which is suitable for playing in an indoor room. Typical examples are string or piano trios, quartets and quintets.

Crescendo – becoming louder.

Diminuendo – becoming quieter.

Effects – Bending: where a musical note played on a string instrument is raised in pitch by pulling or pushing it out of its normal position on the fingerboard. On the guitar, for example, this is achieved by pushing the string upwards or pulling it downwards; using this technique pitches can be altered by microtones, semitones, tones and (especially on electric guitars) even thirds. **Distortion:** an electronic effect used on amplified instruments (particularly electric guitar) which creates a 'dirty', distorted sound that is often used in rock and heavy metal music. **Rolls:** a tremolo (or trill) effect produced on a drum by striking the instrument with two sticks (or beaters) in rapid alternation. **Delay:** an electronic echo effect used on amplified instruments which repeats the notes or phrases played (or sung) by a musician. The delay time can be adjusted. **Reverb**: an electronic effect used to change the acoustic sound of amplified instruments (e.g. can make an instrument sound as though it is in a large concert hall even if it is being played in a small room).

Electronic drums – an electronic device (sometimes called a drum machine) which reproduces drum sounds and rhythmic patterns.

Folk instruments – uillean pipes, banjo, clarsach, bagpipes, accordion, fiddle, whistle, guitar, bodhran.

Gamelan music – a group of musicians from south-east Asia (usually Indonesia) who play their own traditional instruments (gongs, xylophones, metallophones, drums, bowed and plucked strings, oboe, flute) and sing. Gamelan ensembles can range from just a few musicians up to 75, but groups of six singers and 25 players are common. The music is complex and based on a five-note scale (slendro) and a seven-note scale (pelog) from which various other modes are formed.

Ghanaian drum ensemble – a group of musicians from Ghana who play lively dance music using various percussion instruments including drums, shakers, finger bells and ankle bells.

Keyboard instruments – piano, organ, harpsichord, virginal, clavichord, electronic keyboard and synthesizer.

Latin percussion ensemble – a group of percussion musicians who play lively Latin dance music.

Orchestral instruments – the orchestra is split into four groups or 'families' of instruments; these are *woodwind*, *brass*, *percussion* and *strings*. In the woodwind family the standard instruments are flute, oboe, clarinet and bassoon, but piccolo, cor anglais, bass clarinet, saxophone and double bassoon can also be used. The brass family comprises trumpet, French horn, trombone and tuba. Many kinds of instruments can be used in the percussion family, the common tuned instruments being timpani, tubular bells, xylophone and glockenspiel, with untuned instruments including snare drum, gong, cymbals, bass drum, triangle, woodblock and tambourine. The string family is made up of the violin (divided into two groups), viola, cello and double bass.

Panpipes – a hand-held instrument consisting of different lengths of pipes, the tops of which are blown into while the other ends are stopped. This is an ancient instrument which is still used in the folk music of certain countries including Peru, Romania and Burma.

Recorder – a woodwind instrument which dates back to the fourteenth century; there are several types, tuned to different pitches, but the most common are the descant, treble and bass recorders.

Scottish instruments – bagpipes, accordion, fiddle, whistle (penny whistle).

String instruments – violin, viola, cello, double bass, guitars, lute.

Voice ranges (SATB) – *Soprano* (high female voice); *Alto* (low female voice); *Tenor* (high male voice); *Bass* (low male voice).

Intermediate 1 Style/Form Concepts

Blues – an improvised African-American folk music whose name refers to the often melancholy nature of the music and the 'blue' (discordant) notes used. Blues is based on chord progressions which last for 8, 12 or 32 bars (the most common being 12-bar blues) over which a melody normally based on the blues scale is played or sung.

Bothy ballad – a traditional Scottish folk song about hard work and working conditions (often involving farming).

Concerto – a large work, normally in three movements, for a solo instrument and orchestra – e.g. Vivaldi's *The Four Seasons* (for solo violin and orchestra), and Rodrigo's *Concerto de Aranjuez* (for solo guitar and orchestra).

Fanfare – a ceremonial flourish of trumpets or other brass instruments, sometimes with percussion, used for important ceremonies (e.g. royal occasions).

Gaelic Psalms (or 'long tunes') – religious songs from the Western isles of Scotland which can be sung slightly differently by individual members of a church congregation, creating an improvised feel.

Ghanaian – musicians from Ghana who play lively dance music using various percussion instruments including drums, shakers, finger bells and ankle bells. These groups are often referred to as Ghanaian drum ensembles.

Improvisation – inventing music on the spot.

Indonesian gamelan – a group of Indonesian musicians who play their own traditional instruments (gongs, xylophones, metallophones, drums, bowed and plucked strings, oboe, flute) and sometimes also sing. Gamelan ensembles can range from just a few musicians up to 75, but groups of six singers and 25 players are common. The music is complex and based on a five-note scale (slendro) and a seven-note scale (pelog) from which various other modes are formed.

Jig – a fast dance found in Scottish and Irish folk music, normally in 6/8 or 9/8 time.

Mouth music (port a beul) – an improvised vocal style used in place of musical instruments to accompany Scottish dances.

Musical – a popular twentieth-century form of musical theatre, developed from comic opera, with lighthearted, romantic or humorous plots and catchy, up-beat songs as well as spectacular dances and spoken text. Composers of musicals include George Gershwin, Stephen Sondheim and Andrew Lloyd Webber.

Opera – a musical drama which is performed on stage with scenery (like a play) and singers who wear costumes and act out the roles of particular characters. The music (probably the most important part of any opera) is played by an orchestra placed in front of and below the stage (the pit). The two main kinds of opera are *opera seria* (serious opera) and *opera buffa* (comic opera). Famous opera composers include Mozart, Puccini, and Verdi.

Ragtime – a style of popular American music from the early 1900s, characterised by lively, often syncopated melodies in strict rhythm. Most ragtime pieces were written for piano, with many famous examples composed by Scott Joplin (including *The Entertainer* and *Maple Leaf Rag*).

Romantic – the term used to describe the musical style of the nineteenth century, in which composers (such as Mahler, Wagner and Tchaikovsky) created music which explored human feelings and experiences in greater depth than ever before. The music varied from dreamy, romantic or tranquil (e.g. piano miniatures by Chopin and Schumann) to very loud and powerful (e.g. Wagner operas and orchestral works by Holst).

Salsa – a style of lively music from Cuba which appeared in the 1940s, salsa is still a popular kind of dance music in many countries.

Samba – highly syncopated African-Brazilian dance music in *duple metre* (two beats per bar).

Scots ballad – a traditional Scottish folk song in which an unfortunate, sad or important historic story is told (e.g. a death, lost love, disaster or war).

Slow air – a slow tune or song – in traditional Scottish music this could be sung or played on the bagpipes or fiddle.

Swing – a style of lively popular jazz and big band dance music from the 1930s. Pieces by Glenn Miller are among the most famous from the time, as are songs sung by Ella Fitzgerald.

Symphony – a large orchestral work, normally in 3 or 4 movements, which can last for up to an hour or more. A wide variety of musical structures, keys and emotions are often used in the musical journey of a symphony. Composers of symphonies include Mozart, Beethoven and Mahler.

Waulking song – a traditional Scottish Gaelic song which was sung by people (mainly women) while they were doing tedious or repetitive work.

Intermediate 2 (equivalent to Credit Level at Standard Grade)

Intermediate 2 Melody Concepts

Atonal music – music which does not have a specific key but uses any note freely.

Blues scale – a scale based on the pentatonic scale but with the addition of two extra 'blue' notes (semitones which create brief discord), e.g. C E$\flat$ F F$\sharp$ G B$\flat$ C C$\sharp$. Used in blues music.

Grace note – a musical 'ornament': a rapid additional note used to decorate a melody.

Interval – the distance between two notes (e.g. C to G is a fifth; G to B is a third).

Melismatic word setting – where several notes are sung to a single syllable in vocal music – as in early religious plainsong.

Modulating – where a piece of music begins to change to another key.

Relative major – a major key which is related to a minor key because it has the same key signature (all minor keys have relative major keys).

Relative minor – a minor key which is related to a major key because it has the same key signature (all major keys have relative minor keys).

Syllabic word setting – where only one note is sung to every syllable in vocal music – the opposite of melismatic music.

Tonal music – music which uses a specific key (or keys) and therefore has a key note.

Trill – an ornament where two notes a semitone or a tone apart alternate rapidly with each other.

Whole-tone scale – a scale which moves only in tones (e.g. C D E F♯ G♯ B♭ C).

Word painting – a technique used mainly in the sixteenth century and the Baroque period where music is used to describe the words in a direct way (e.g. the word *misery* could be accompanied by a sad minor chord, or a loud drum might play when the word *thunder* is sung).

Intermediate 2 Harmony Concepts

Chord progressions using chords I, IV, V and VI – the ability to use (in compositions) and recognise (by ear) chord changes between chords I, IV, V and VI in major and minor keys.

Consonance – when musical notes sounding together are harmonious or 'pleasing' to the ear – for example, intervals of a third, fourth, fifth or octave are consonant.

Dissonance – when musical notes sounding together are not harmonious, creating a discord or even a jarring and unpleasant sound – for example, intervals such as seconds or sevenths. Dissonance is effective in creating tension, drama, unrest, even horror!

Imperfect cadence – where a passage of music does not end with the key chord, creating the feeling that the phrase or section is unfinished. The most common imperfect cadences are chord I to chord V, and chord I to chord IV.

Interval – the distance between two notes (e.g. C to G is a fifth; G to B is a third).

Modulation – when music changes from one key to another.

Modulation to relative minor – when music in a major key changes to the relative minor key (for example, a piece in G major would modulate to E minor).

Passing note – a note which appears in between two notes (normally a third apart) to create a smooth, stepwise movement (e.g. the note D would be a passing note between C and E to produce: C D E).

Perfect cadence – where a passage of music ends with the key chord (chord I), creating the feeling that the phrase or section is finished. The most common perfect cadences are chord V to chord I and chord IV to chord I.

Suspension – where a note is held on from a chord to create brief dissonance in the chord which follows, before resolving itself again in the third chord.

Tierce de Picardie – a technique commonly used in the sixteenth century and Baroque periods where a piece of music in a minor key/mode ends on the major chord (e.g. a piece in A minor finishes with an A major chord).

Intermediate 2 Rhythm Concepts

Cross rhythms – where the normal accents of a time signature are moved around to create different kinds of rhythms in a piece of music, or when separate parts play different rhythms at the same time.

Dotted rhythms – a distinctive rhythm produced by the addition of a dot after a note, which increases the time value of that note by half. Well-known melodies which use dotted rhythms are *Auld Lang Syne* and the Christmas carol *The First Nowell*.

Rhythmic groupings in simple and compound time – the specific ways in which notes are grouped together in simple time signatures (such as 2/2, 2/4, 3/4, 3/8 and 4/4) and compound time signatures (such as 6/8, 9/8 and 12/8).

Triplets – where three notes are to be played in the time of a single beat. For example, Where triplets occur, they are normally indicated by the addition of the number 3 above the notes.

Intermediate 2 Structure Concepts

Alberti bass – a broken chord pattern which is used as a bass accompaniment; the pattern is often: *lowest note of chord – highest note of chord – middle note of chord – highest note of chord* (e.g. C G E G).

Cadenza – a complex section for the soloist (which shows his/her skill) near the end of a concerto movement or an aria.

Coda – a short 'ending' section which concludes a piece of music.

Contrapuntal (Counterpoint) – where two different musical parts (which sound complete in themselves) are played simultaneously to create a single, harmonious piece – a popular style in the Baroque period, but used by composers ever since.

Countermelody – a second melody which complements the main melody and usually has a different rhythm, as in counterpoint.

Ground bass – a bass melody or motif which is constantly repeated.

Homophony – where voices or instruments sounding together move in the same rhythm.

Inverted pedal – a note which is sustained or constantly repeated in a high part while other parts below it change.

Obbligato – a separate instrumental part which, although secondary to the main melody, forms a distinct melodic accompaniment and must not be left out of the music.

Pedal – a note which is held (sustained) or constantly repeated in the bass while other parts above it change.

Polyphony – where two or more voices or instruments sound together but have different rhythms – the term evolved in the sixteenth-century Renaissance period.

Strophic – a term used to describe vocal music in which different lyrics are sung to the same musical verse each time.

Through-composed – a term used to describe a song where the music changes in each verse or stanza, or a piece of instrumental music with no definite form.

Intermediate 2 Timbre Concepts

12-string guitar – an acoustic guitar with six standard main strings, underneath each of which is an extra thinner string which adds extra resonance and volume to the instrument.

A cappella – a term used to describe unaccompanied choral music.

Arco – 'bow': an instruction to players of bowed string instruments to go back to playing with the bow after a pizzicato section.

Baritone – the male voice range between bass and tenor.

Col legno – 'with the wood': an instruction to players of bowed string instruments to play the strings using the wood of the bow – this creates a staccato effect.

Con sordino – 'with the mute': an instruction to string and brass players to mute their sound.

Counter tenor – the high or 'falsetto' male voice range between tenor and alto.

Double-stopping – playing two notes at the same time on a stringed instrument such as violin, cello, or guitar.

Flutter-tonguing – a technique used by wind players (especially on the flute) where the tongue rolls the letter 'r' to create a kind of tremolo effect.

Fretless bass guitar – a bass guitar which, unlike a standard bass guitar, has no frets. Rather like a cello, the fretless bass requires the player to judge where each string has to be stopped to produce particular notes.

Glissando – to slide smoothly between two notes which are some distance apart, with all the notes in between being played very rapidly.

Mezzo-soprano – the female voice range between soprano and alto.

Muted – dampening the sound produced by an instrument to make it quieter; this can be done with the hand on some instruments (such as guitar and French horn), or by using a special device known as a mute (on orchestral stringed instruments and brass instruments).

Pizzicato – an instruction to string players to pluck the strings with the fingers instead of using the bow.

Register – a particular pitch range of a group of notes, instrument or voice (e.g. a high register for the violin would be notes which use ledger lines above the treble stave).

Sitar – a large acoustic Indian instrument which resembles a guitar with a very long neck. It has twenty moveable frets and seven main strings underneath which are normally another twelve 'sympathetic' strings tuned by pegs along the fingerboard.

Slide guitar – a guitar with steel strings where the player plucks or picks the strings in the normal way with one hand, but uses a slide (a hollow tube usually made of glass or chrome) worn on a finger of the other hand to slide along the strings and produce different pitches; this creates a smooth and characteristic sound commonly associated with blues music.

Tabla – a pair of hand-played drums (one treble, one bass) used mainly in Indian music.

Tremolando/Tremolo – the very rapid repetition of a single note to create a trembling effect.

Vibrato – a technique used by singers and players of stringed instruments where a rapid fluctuation in the pitch of a note is produced, creating the effect that the note is vibrating or swaying gently.

Intermediate 2 Style/Form Concepts

Aleatoric – a twentieth-century style which describes music in which some (or all) parts of the composition or performance are left to chance, e.g. the composer might roll dice to determine which bar numbers will contain a particular melody, or allow the player the freedom to play a set of given notes in any order or rhythm.

Aria – a song, especially from an opera or oratario.

Boogie-woogie – a blues piano style from the early twentieth century characterised by a repetitive bass rhythm (played by the left hand) over which an improvised melody is played (with the right hand).

Cantata – a large vocal work (often religious) for chorus and orchestra, especially popular in the Baroque period.

Chorale – a congregational hymn tune of the Lutheran (German) church. Composers such as J S Bach built more complex pieces of music around these basic hymn tunes.

Chorus – a large group of singers who perform together, often divided into parts for different voice ranges.

Classical – the term used to describe music which is not part of folk or popular traditions, as well as music from the late eighteenth to early nineteenth centuries where careful attention to detail, formal structures (such as the sonata and symphony) and general high standards of musical excellence were the aim of composers including Haydn, Mozart and Beethoven.

Country – a style of popular American folk music which was first played in rural communities at functions or in the home (using fiddles, banjos and guitars) but later expanded into a large industry where the style was developed by performers such as Willie Nelson, Patsy Cline, Dolly Parton and Johnny Cash.

Dixieland – an early style of traditional jazz music from the USA played by white musicians of the so-called 'New Orleans School'.

Hymn tune – a religious devotional song normally sung by church congregations.

Impressionist – a style, first appearing in the 1870s, where the expression of a mood (often dreamy and romantic) or an emotion is the most important aspect, and musical structures and chord progressions are looser.

Indian – all styles of Indian music, which include vocal music, Indian classical music and instrumental styles. Indian melodies are formed using special scales/modes called ragas and various set rhythmic patterns known as talas.

Minimalist – a term first used in the early 1970s to describe music which uses simple, repetitive melodies and rhythms that are gradually extended by adding more and more of these simple 'layers' of music until a more complex structure develops.

Oratorio – a large musical setting of a religious text involving choir, soloists and orchestra; similar to opera, but without acting, costumes or scenery.

Passion – a piece which portrays the story of the crucifixion of Jesus Christ. Over the centuries there have been several versions of this style, but its largest is an orchestral work with chorus and soloists; Bach's *St John Passion* and *St Matthew Passion* are considered the finest examples.

Pibroch – a term for more serious and complex highland bagpipe music – pibrochs use a theme and variation structure.

Recitative – a speech in an opera which is sung in a way which follows the natural pitch and rhythms of spoken words (creating a kind of half-sung, half-spoken effect).

Scherzo – a lively, playful instrumental movement which is usually part of a larger work such as a sonata or symphony and is often paired with a trio section.

Soul – a style of popular music from African-American musicians since the early 1960s where the performer displays strong and sincere emotions through a very expressive singing style.

ANSWERS TO LISTENING EXERCISES

Chapter 1: Chords and Cadences

Part 1: Chord Identification

Listening Exercise 1: **CD track 1** Dominant 7th chord

Listening Exercise 2: **CD track 2** Diminished chord

Listening Exercise 3: **CD track 3** Diminished 7th chord

Listening Exercise 4: **CD track 4** Added 6th chord

Listening Exercise 5: **CD track 5** Diminished 7th chord

Listening Exercise 6: **CD track 6** Augmented chord

Part 2: Cadence Identification

Listening Exercise 7: **CD track 7** Imperfect cadence

Listening Exercise 8: **CD track 8** Perfect cadence

Listening Exercise 9: **CD track 9** Interrupted cadence

Listening Exercise 10: **CD track 10** Plagal cadence

Listening Exercise 11: **CD track 11** Imperfect cadence

Listening Exercise 12: **CD track 12** Interrupted cadence

Chapter 2: Renaissance Music

Listening Exercise 13: **CD track 13**
- ☑ Air
- ☑ Chromatic notes
- ☑ Syncopation

Listening Exercise 14: **CD track 14**
- ☑ Madrigal
- ☑ Imitative polyphony
- ☑ Melismatic word setting

Listening Exercise 15: **CD track 15**
- ☑ Pavan
- ☑ Consort
- ☑ Major tonality

Listening Exercise 16: **CD track 16**

- ☑ Syllabic word setting
- ☑ Ballett
- ☑ Homophony

Listening Exercise 17: **CD track 17**

- ☑ Mass
- ☑ Melismatic word setting
- ☑ Polyphony

Listening Exercise 18: **CD track 18**

- ☑ Triple metre (3/4)
- ☑ Galliard
- ☑ Consort

Listening Exercise 19: **CD track 19**

- ☑ Plainchant
- ☑ Antiphonal
- ☑ Legato
- ☑ Mode

Listening Exercise 20: **CD track 20**

- ☑ Descant
- ☑ Motet
- ☑ Polyphony
- ☑ Rallentando

Chapter 3: Baroque Music

Listening Exercise 21: CD track 21

(a) ☑ Basso continuo
 ☑ Concerto grosso
 ☑ Modulation
 ☑ Perfect cadence

(b) Turn

(c) (i) Ripieno
 (ii) Concertino

Listening Exercise 22: CD track 22

- ☑ Passion
- ☑ Tierce de Picardie
- ☑ Homophony
- ☑ Suspension

Listening Exercise 23: CD track 23

(a) ☑ Overture

   ☑ Drone bass/pedal

   ☑ Trill

   ☑ Dotted rhythms

(b) ☑ The time signature changes from simple time to compound time

(c) Timpani

Listening Exercise 24: CD track 24

(a) ☑ Chorale prelude

   ☑ Mordent

   ☑ Tierce de Picardie

   ☑ Countermelody

(b) Organ

(c) Harpsichord **or** Clavichord **or** Virginal

Listening Exercise 25: CD track 25

☑ Modulation

☑ Minuet

☑ Walking bass

☑ Basso continuo

Listening Exercise 26: CD track 26

(a) ☑ Countersubject

   ☑ Answer

   ☑ Stretto

   ☑ Fugue

Listening Exercise 26: CD track 27

(b) Minor

(c) Harpsichord

(d) ☑ Canon

Listening Exercise 27: CD track 28

The excerpt opens with __STRINGS/VIOLINS__ playing a melody which begins not on the first beat of the bar, but with an __ANACRUSIS__. One of the accompanying instruments is cello, which sometimes can be heard repeating the same bass note to create a __PEDAL__. Also accompanying is a harpsichord; this instrument was often used as an accompaniment instrument in Baroque music in a part of the orchestra known as the __BASSO CONTINUO__. After a section where a second melodic idea or theme is played, and then repeated, there follows a passage played by solo violins. Two ornaments used by the violins in this passage are an __ACCIACCATURA__ and a __TRILL__. Another technique is used where the violinists, instead of changing the bow direction for each note, play two or more notes with a single up-bow or down-bow. This common string technique is known as __SLURS/SLURRING__. When the solo violin passage is finished, the larger instrumental group or full orchestra enter again, repeating one of the melodic themes played earlier. This particular melodic theme is repeated several times throughout the piece by the main instrumental group and is known as a __RITORNELLO.__ The style/form of the piece is a __CONCERTO__.

Listening Exercise 28: CD track 29

(a) ☑ Rallentando

☑ Antiphonal

☑ Perfect cadence

☑ Oratorio

(b) (i) Trumpet

(ii) Timpani

(c) Both instruments play in rhythmic unison

(d) ☑ Homophonic SATB

Listening Exercise 29: CD track 30

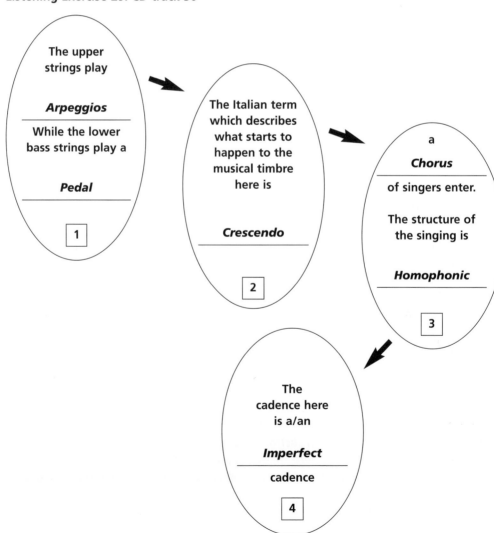

The upper strings play

Arpeggios

While the lower bass strings play a

Pedal

1

The Italian term which describes what starts to happen to the musical timbre here is

Crescendo

2

a

Chorus

of singers enter.

The structure of the singing is

Homophonic

3

The cadence here is a/an

Imperfect

cadence

4

Chapter 4: Classical and Romantic Music

Listening Exercise 30: CD track 31

(a) ☑ Trill

☑ Melodic sequence

☑ Harmonic sequence

☑ Alberti bass

(b) Exposition

(c) (i) Imperfect cadence

(ii) Perfect cadence

Listening Exercise 31: CD track 32

(a) ☑ Appoggiatura

☑ Chamber music

☑ Anacrusis

☑ Repetition

(b) Compound duple (or 6/8)

(c) 1. Piano

2. Violin

3. Cello

Listening Exercise 31: CD track 33

(a) ☑ Inverted pedal

☑ Chromatic notes

☑ Imitation

☑ Acciaccatura

(b) Imperfect cadence

(c) Classical

(d) ☑ Modulation

Listening Exercise 32: CD track 34

(a) ☑ Staccato

☑ Crescendo

☑ Imitation

(b) Canon

(c) (i) Symphony

(ii) Classical

(d) ☑ Scherzo

Listening Exercise 33: CD track 35

☑ Chromatic notes

☑ Imitation

☑ Impressionism

☑ Pedal

Listening Exercise 34: CD track 36

☑ Repetition

☑ Acciaccatura

☑ Modal

☑ Rhythmic ostinato

Listening Exercise 35: CD track 37

(a) ☑ Recitative

   ☑ Aria

   ☑ Coloratura

   ☑ Staccato

(b) Opera

(c) Perfect cadence

(d) ☑ Classical

Listening Exercise 36: CD track 38

(a) ☑ Descending chromatic scale

   ☑ Trill

   ☑ Staccato

   ☑ Ascending chromatic scale

(b) Concerto

(c) ☑ Triplets

Listening Exercise 37: CD tracks 39 and 40

CONCEPTS	EXCERPT 1 (Track 39)	EXCERPT 2 (Track 40)	COMMON TO BOTH EXCERPTS
TIMBRE Col legno			
Coloratura			
Sprechgesang			
Bass voice			
Tenor voice			✓
HARMONIC Interrupted cadence			
Modulation			✓
Suspension			
Diminished 7th chord			
Major tonality			✓
STRUCTURAL Inverted pedal			
Compound time		✓	
Alberti bass			
Through-composed			
Rhythmic ostinato		✓	
STYLES/FORMS Recitative			
Cantata			
Aria	✓		
Lied		✓	
Opera	✓		
	2 marks	3 marks	3 marks

Listening Exercise 38: CD track 41

(a) ☑ Symphonic/Tone poem

    ☑ Legato

    ☑ Pizzicato

(b) French horn

(c) (i) Bassoon

    (ii) Cor anglais (Oboe also acceptable)

Listening Exercise 39: CD track 42

(a) ☑ Accelerando

☑ Accents

☑ Hemiola

(b) (i) Cymbals **or** Timpani **or** Triangle

(ii) Cymbals **or** Timpani **or** Triangle

(c) Nationalism

Listening Exercise 40: CD track 43

☑ Arpeggios

☑ Pedal

☑ Programmatic

☑ Sequence

Listening Exercise 41: CD track 44

(a) ☑ Sequence

☑ Three against two

☑ Imitation

(b) Romantic

(c) Symphony

(d) Cymbals

Chapter 5: Twentieth-century Music

Listening Exercise 42: CD track 45

☑ Pause (fermata)

☑ Tremolando/Tremolo

☑ Timpani roll

☑ Crescendo

Listening Exercise 43: CD track 46

(a) ☑ Minimalism

☑ Snare drum

☑ Triangle

☑ Timpani

(b) Violin

(c) Legato

(d) ☑ Concerto

Listening Exercise 44: CD track 47

(a) ☑ Atonal

☑ Flutter tonguing

☑ Staccato

(b) Rubato

(c) Trill

(d) ☑ Diminuendo

Listening Exercise 45: CD track 48

(a) ☑ Tabla

☑ Microtone

☑ Improvisation

☑ Bending

(b) Sitar

(c) Indian

Listening Exercise 46: CD track 49

(a) ☑ Symphony

☑ Diminuendo

☑ Sequence

☑ Tremolando/Tremolo strings

(b) Roll (or Trill)

(c) Imperfect cadence

Listening Exercise 47: CD track 50

☑ Atonal

☑ Opera

☑ Sprechgesang

☑ Pizzicato

Listening Exercise 48: CD track 51

(a) ☑ Cross rhythms

☑ Triangle

☑ Polytonality

☑ Dissonance

(b) Snare drum **or** Timpani **or** Bass drum

(c) Piccolo

Listening Exercise 49: CD track 52

☑ Melodic sequence

☑ Delay

☑ Bass guitar riff

☑ Backing vocals

Listening Exercise 50: CD track 53

☑ Improvisation

☑ Ostinato

☑ Gamelan

Listening Exercise 51: CD track 54

(a) ☑ Polytonality

☑ Trill

☑ Cross rhythms

(b) Accelerando

(c) (i) Piano

(ii) Snare or Bass drum

(d) ☑ Clarinet

Chapter 6: Musical Literacy

Musical Literacy Exercise 1: CD track 55

(i)

(ii) see notation below

(iii) see notation below

(iv) 7

(v) see notation below

(vi) see notation below

Supplementary Questions for Musical Literacy Exercise 1

(i) Acciaccatura

(ii) Three times

(iii) A third

(iv) Natural and sharp

(v) Staccato dots

(vi) They both have the same rhythm, but bar 6 is pitched a sixth lower than bar 2, and bars 7 and 8 are pitched a fourth lower than bars 3 and 4

Musical Literacy Exercise 2: CD track 56

(i)

(ii) see notation below

(iii) 2
4

(iv) see notation below

(v) Bars 3 and 4

Contrary motion

(vi) see notation below

First Violins

Supplementary Questions for Musical Literacy Exercise 2

(i) Bars 5 and 6

(ii) Imperfect cadence

(iii) A seventh

(iv) Quaver (or eighth note) rest

(v) Four

(vi) Bar 2

Answers

HOW TO PASS HIGHER MUSIC LISTENING

Musical Literacy Exercise 3: CD track 57

(i)

(ii) see notation below

(iii) see notation below

(iv) 4
     4

(v) The first five notes of bars 10–11 are the same as the notes in bars 8 and 9, only one octave higher in pitch; these notes also have the same rhythm.

(vi) see notation below

Supplementary Questions for Musical Literacy Exercise 3

(i) Syncopation

(ii) Classical guitars

(iii) Major

(iv) Broken chord

(v) Lowest note: D   Highest note: F

Interval: compound third

(vi) Pause (fermata). Indicates that the player should pause on this note (sustain it for longer than its written value).

Musical Literacy Exercise 4: CD track 58

(i) Turn (or, *inverted Turn*, bar 3, *Turn,* bar 6, and *Inverted Turn* bar 11)

(ii) see notation below

(iii) Quaver (or eighth note) rest

(iv) 2
4

(v) 7

(vi) see notation below

Supplementary Questions for Musical Literacy Exercise 4

(i)   These notes should be played one octave higher than written

(ii) Pedal

(iii) Bars 1–2, bars 4–7, bar 8 and bar 10

(iv) The sustain pedal on the piano should be used here

(v)   see notation on previous page

(vi) see notation on previous page

Musical Literacy Exercise 5: CD track 59

(i)

(ii) see notation below

(iii) see notation below

(iv) 6

(v)   Bars 6 and 7

(vi) see notation below

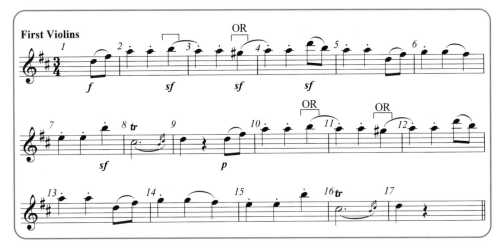

Supplementary Questions for Musical Literacy Exercise 5

(i)   Bars 5 and 13

(ii) Perfect cadence

(iii) Trill

(iv) Double grace note

(v)   Anacrusis

(vi) Bars 9–17 are an exact repeat of bars 1–9, but played softer

Musical Literacy Exercise 6: CD track 60

(i)

(ii) see notation below

(iii) see notation below

(iv) Accent

(v) Trill

(vi) Bar 21

Supplementary Questions for Musical Literacy Exercise 6

(i) Everyone (the whole orchestra play together)

(ii) Concerto

(iii) Bar 3

(iv) Five

(v) Imitation (or Repetition)

(vi) Four (bars 21 and 23)

Musical Literacy Exercise 7: CD track 61

(i)

(ii) see notation below

(iii) Melodic sequence

(iv) Bars 11–18 repeat bars 3–10 one octave higher

(v) Slurs and Staccato

(vi) see notation below

First Violins

Supplementary Questions for Musical Literacy Exercise 7

(i)   Two octaves

(ii) Five (bars 3, 4, 5, 6 and 10)

(iii) Pedal or drone bass

(iv) Four

(v) see notation above

(vi) Cut Time: 2/2 time

Musical Literacy Exercise 8: CD track 62

(i)

(ii) see notation below

(iii) see notation below

(iv) (a) Third

   (b) Second

   (c) Fourth

   (d) Octave

(v) 9

(vi) see notation below

Supplementary Questions for Musical Literacy Exercise 8

(i) The second violins part at bar 14 has the same rhythm as both violin parts in bar 1, and also uses staccato

(ii) Sequence

(iii) (a) Ties

(b) Slurs

(iv) Crescendo (gradually louder)

(v) Bar 7

(vi) Suddenly loud, going to very soft

Chapter 7: Specimen Listening Question Paper

Question 1: CD track 63

(a) ☑ Guitar riff

☑ Backing vocals

☑ Syllabic word setting

☑ Glissando

(b) Bongo drums

(c) Soul

Question 2: CD track 64

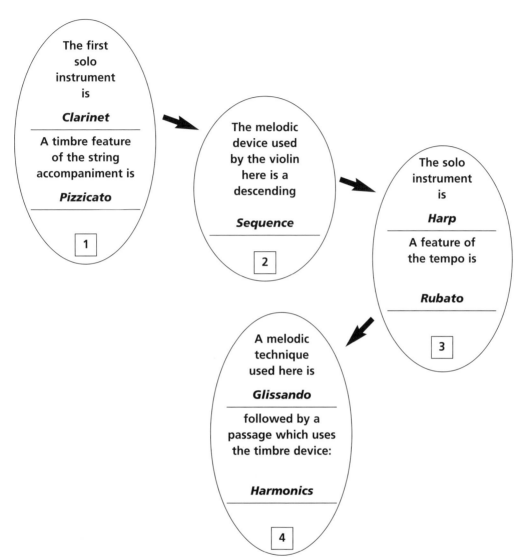

The first solo instrument is

Clarinet

A timbre feature of the string accompaniment is

Pizzicato

1

The melodic device used by the violin here is a descending

Sequence

2

The solo instrument is

Harp

A feature of the tempo is

Rubato

3

A melodic technique used here is

Glissando

followed by a passage which uses the timbre device:

Harmonics

4

Question 3: CD track 65

☑ Hemiola
☑ Renaissance
☑ Galliard

Question 4: CD track 66

(i)

(ii) see notation below

(iii) see notation below

(iv) Bar 8

(v)   Bars 4 and 5

(vi) see notation below

Question 5: CD track 67

(a) ☑ Cantata

    ☑ Sequence

    ☑ Melismatic word setting

(b) Oboe

(c) (i) Bassoon

    (ii) Staccato

(d) ☑ Baritone

Question 6: CD track 68

The first instrument to be heard playing the melody is a/an <u>OBOE</u>, and an ornament used by this instrument is a <u>TURN</u>. The rising and falling phrase structure of the melody could be described as <u>QUESTION</u> and <u>ANSWER</u> phrases. The second woodwind instrument to enter playing the melody is <u>FLUTE</u>. A passage of music then follows in which both of these woodwind instruments share the melody by alternating with each other and also playing in <u>UNISON</u>. Another ornament heard in this section of music is a/an <u>TRILL</u>, and a melodic device used is <u>SEQUENCE</u>. The Italian term which describes how the music slows down at the end of this passage is <u>RALLENTANDO (rall.) (or RITARDANDO (rit.))</u>. A livelier section of music then begins in which the time signature changes to <u>6/8 (or COMPOUND)</u> time from previously being in <u>2/2 (or SIMPLE or 4/4)</u> time. Although the melody changes in this new section, it is based on that of the previous section; this technique is known as <u>VARIATION</u>. Written by Stravinsky in 1920, this piece was composed in the earlier style of classical music; the style or structure of this composition would therefore be referred to as <u>NEO-CLASSICAL</u>.

Question 7: CD tracks 69 and 70

CONCEPTS	EXCERPT 1 (Track 69)	EXCERPT 2 (Track 70)	COMMON TO BOTH EXCERPTS
MELODIC Trill			✓
Vibrato	✓		
Atonal			
Triplets		✓	
Microtone			
HARMONIC Interrupted cadence			
Tierce de Picardie			
Polytonality			
Pizzicato			✓
Cluster chords			
STRUCTURAL Inverted pedal			
Ostinato			
Cadenza		✓	
Aria			
Polyphonic			
STYLES/FORMS Baroque			
Classical		✓	
Romantic	✓		
Symphony			
Concerto			✓
	2 marks	3 marks	3 marks

CD TRACK LIST

CD track	Title	Composer (Performers)	Recording Co.	Page
1	**Adagio molto e cantabile** (Movement 3 from Symphony no. 9)	**Beethoven** *(Berlin Philharmonic Orchestra; Ferenc Fricsay)*	Deutsche Grammophon **463 626-2**	10
2	**Exsamplin'**	**Joe McGowan**	Hodder Gibson	10
3	**Kriegers Ahnung** (from Schwanengesang)	**Franz Schubert** *(András Schiff (piano))*	The Decca Record Company Limited **00289 475 2682**	10
4	**We are the Champ**	**Armath & J. Deja** *(Joe McGowan)*	Hodder Gibson	10
5	**Allegro Moderato** (Movement 1 from Piano Concerto no. 4)	**Beethoven** *(Claudio Arrau, piano; Royal Concertgebouw Orchestra, Amsterdam; Bernard Haitink)*	Philips Classics (Universal) **468 113-2**	10
6	**Body and Soul**	**John Green** *(Joe McGowan)*	Hodder Gibson	11
7	**Allegro** (Movement 1 from Symphony no. 104)	**Haydn** *(London Philharmonic Orchestra; Sir Georg Solti)*	The Decca Record Company Limited **417 330-2**	12
8	**Allegro ma non troppo** (Movement I from Symphony no. 9)	**Beethoven** *(Berlin Philharmonic Orchestra; Ferenc Fricsay)*	Deutsche Grammophon **463 626-2**	12
9	**Adagio** (Movement 2 from Clarinet Concerto in A major K622)	**Mozart** *(English Chamber Orchestra)*	AVIE Records **AV0035**	12
10	**Adagio cantabile** (Movement 3 from Symphony no. 2)	**Charles Ives** *(Nashville Symphony Orchestra; Kenneth Schermerhorn)*	Naxos **8.559076**	12

CD track	Title	Composer (Performers)	Recording Co.	Page
11	Aria: 'Rollend in schäumenden Wellen' (from The Creation)	**Haydn** (Gerald Finley; English Baroque Soloists; John Eliot Gardiner)	**Archiv Produktion Deutsche Grammophon 449 217-2**	13
12	Largo, 'Sento dire no'ncè pace' (from Pulcinella)	**Stravinsky** (Teresa Berganza; Ryland Davies; John Shirley-Quirk; London Symphony Orchestra; Claudio Abbado)	**Deutsche Grammophon 453 085-2**	13
13	All ye whom love or fortune	**John Dowland** (Catherine King; Jacob Heringman, lute)	**Naxos 8.553326**	16
14	Vezzosi augelli	**G. Wert** (Amaryllis Consort)	**IMP Red Label PCD 822**	17
15	Mr John Langton's Pavan	**John Dowland** (Rose consort of viols; Jacob Heringman, lute)	**Naxos 8.553326**	17
16	Now is the Month of Maying	**Thomas Morley** (Arr. P Rosseter, Dowland Consort; Jakob Lindberg)	**BIS (Naxos) BIS-CD-451**	17
17	Agnus Dei II	**Palestrina** (Christ Church Cathedral Choir; director, Stephen Darlington)	**Nimbus Records Limited NI 5100**	17
18	The King of Denmark's Galliard	**John Dowland** (Rose consort of viols; Jacob Heringman, lute)	**Naxos 8.553326**	18
19	Kyrie	**Traditional** (monasteries of France)	**Music Collection International MCCD 130**	18
20	Motet: Dum complerentur dies pentecostes	**Palestrina** (Christ Church Cathedral Choir; director, Stephen Darlington)	**Nimbus Records Limited NI 5100**	18
21	Minuetto (vivace) (from Concerto grosso in C, Op. 6, no. 10)	**A. Corelli** (The English Concert; Trevor Pinnock)	**Polydor International Archiv Produktion (Deutsche Grammophon) 459 451-2**	23

CD track	Title	Composer (Performers)	Recording Co.	Page
22	Choral: 'O große Lieb, o Lieb ohn' alle Maße' (from the *St John Passion*)	J S Bach (Monteverdi Choir; *English Baroque Soloists; John Eliot Gardiner*)	Archiv Produktion Polydor International 419 324-2	23
23	Ouverture IV (from Suite no. 4 in D, BWV 1069)	J S Bach (*English Concert; Trevor Pinnock*)	Deutsche Grammophon 463 013-2	23
24	Das alte Jahr vergangen ist BWV 1091	J S Bach (*Hans Fagius, organ*)	BIS (Naxos) BIS-CD-379-80	24
25	Minuet (from Suite no.1 in C, BWV 1066)	J S Bach (*English Concert; Trevor Pinnock*)	Deutsche Grammophon 463 013-2	24
26	Fugue no. 19 in A major BWV 864	J S Bach (*Luc Beausejour*)	Naxos 8.55762526	25
27	Canon 4 a 2 per Augmentationem contrario motu (from the *Musical Offering*)	J S Bach (*Christian Benda; Sebastian Benda; Kramer; Nils; Thilo; Pfister; Ariane; Capella Istropolitana*)	Naxos 8.553286	25
28	Allegro (Movement 1 from 'Spring', *The Four Seasons*)	Vivaldi (*I Solisti Italiani*)	Union Square Music Ltd SIMPLYCD003-1	26
29	Praise the Lord (from *Solomon*)	Handel (*English Baroque Soloists; Monteverdi Choir; John Eliot Gardiner*)	Philips Classics (Universal) 468 151-2	26
30	Zadok the Priest	Handel (*Chorus and Academy of St Martin-in-the-Fields; Sir Neville Marriner*)	Philips Classics (Universal) 468 151-2	27
31	Allegro (from piano sonata no.15 in C major, K545)	Mozart (*Jenö Jandó*)	Naxos 8.554908DX	32
32	Allegro (Piano Trio in G major, K564)	Mozart (*Borodin Trio*)	Chandos digital CHAN 8536(2)	32
33	Allegro (Piano Trio in G major, K564)	Mozart (*Borodin Trio*)	Chandos digital CHAN 8536(2)	32

CD track	Title	Composer (Performers)	Recording Co.	Page
34	Molto vivace (Movement 2 from Symphony no. 9)	Beethoven (Berlin Philharmonic Orchestra; Ferenc Fricsay)	Deutsche Grammophon 463 626-2	33
35	Prelude a l'apres-midi d'un faune	Claude Debussy (Jan van Reeth; BRT Philharmonic Orchestra, Brussels; Alexander Rahbari)	Naxos 8.550262	34
36	Gnossienne 1	Eric Satie (Yuji Takahashi, piano)	Union Square Music Ltd SIMPLYCD003-4	34
37	'Il capro e la capretta' (from The Marriage of Figaro)	Mozart (Terfel; Hagley; Martinpelto; Gilfry; Stephen; McCulloch; Feller; The Monteverdi Choir; The English Baroque Soloists; John Eliot Gardener)	Archiv Produktion (Deutsche Grammophon) 439 871-2	35
38	Allegro Moderato (Movement 1 from Piano Concerto no. 4)	Beethoven (Claudio Arrau, piano; Royal Concertgebouw Orchestra Amsterdam; Bernard Haitink)	Philips Classics Universal 468 113-2	35
39	'Isolde! Geliebte! – Tristan! Geliebter!' (from Tristan and Isolde)	Richard Wagner (Carlos Kleiber)	Deutsche Grammophon 477 535-5	36
40	Das Fischermädchen (from Schwanengesang)	Franz Schubert (Peter Schreier (tenor); András Schiff (piano))	The Decca Record Company Limited 00289 475 2682	36
41	Romeo and Juliet Fantasy Overture	Tchaikovsky (Moscow Radio Symphony Orchestra)	DGR Records RINGO326B	39
42	Slavonic Dance in C Major Op. 46, no. 1	Dvořák (Sudwest Orchestra; Karl August Niecks)	DGR Records RINGO326A	39
43	Aquarium (from Le Carnaval des Animaux)	C. Saint-Saëns (Martha Argerich; Mischa Maisky; Gidon Kremer; Isabelle van Keulen; Tabe Zimmerman; Georg Hörtnagel)	Deutsche Grammophon 469 310-2	40

CD track	Title	Composer (Performers)	Recording Co.	Page
44	Allegro (Movement 3 from Symphony no. 3 in C minor, Op. 78, 'Organ Symphony')	Saint Saëns (Orchestre de l'Opéra Bastille; Myung-Whun Chung)	Deutsche Grammophon 435 854-2	40
45	Movement 1 (Symphony no. 6)	Jean Sibelius (Berlin Philharmonic Orchestra; Herbert von Karajan)	Deutsche Grammophon 474 353-2	45
46	Movement 3 (from Concerto for Violin and Orchestra)	Philip Glass (Gidon Kremer, violin; Vienna Philharmonic Orchestra; Christoph Von Dohnányi)	Deutsche Grammophon 445 185-2	45
47	Explosion 1 (from 'In Freundschaft')	Karlheinz Stockhausen (Christian Lindberg)	Naxos Label: BIS BIS-CD-388	45
48	Rāga Pūriyā-Kalyān	Traditional (Pandit Ravi Shankar)	Ocora Radio France C 558674 HM 90	46
49	Lento Maestoso (Movement 4 from Symphony no. 2)	Charles Ives (Nashville Symphony Orchestra; Kenneth Schermerhorn)	Naxos 8.559076	46
50	Einziger, ewiger, allgegenwärtiger (from Moses and Aaron)	Arnold Schoenberg (David Pittman-Jennings; Chorus Of The Netherlands Opera; Zaans Jongenskoor; Royal Concertgebouw Orchestra; Pierre Boulez)	Deutsche Grammophon 449 174-2	47
51	The Gong on the Hook and Ladder or Firemen's Parade on Main Street	Charles Ives (Ensemble Modern; Ingo Metzmacher)	EMI CDC7 5455-2	47
52	Flaming Star	Sally Oldfield	New World Music Ltd NWCD 506	47
53	Bendrong	Traditional	Topic Records Ltd TSCD913	48
54	Central Park in the Dark	Charles Ives (Gulbenkian Orchestra; Michel Swierczewski)	Nimbus Records 5316	48

CD track	Title	Composer (Performers)	Recording Co.	Page
55	Allegro Moderato (Movement 1 from Piano Concerto no. 4)	Beethoven (Claudio Arrau, piano; Royal Concertgebouw Orchestra, Amsterdam; Bernard Haitink)	Philips Classics (Universal) 468 113-2	50
56	Andante (Movement 2 from Symphony no. 104)	Haydn (London Philharmonic Orchestra; Sir Georg Solti)	The Decca Record Company Limited 417 330-2	52
57	The Girl From Ipanema	Antonio Carlos Jobim (Joe McGowan and Cameron Angus)	Hodder Gibson	53
58	Rondo (Movement 3 from Piano Concerto no. 4)	Beethoven (Claudio Arrau, piano; Royal Concertgebouw Orchestra, Amsterdam; Bernard Haitink)	Philips Classics (Universal) 468 113-2	55
59	Menuetto (Movement 3 from Symphony no. 104)	Haydn (London Philharmonic Orchestra; Sir Georg Solti)	The Decca Record Company Limited 417 330-2	56
60	Rondo (Movement 3 from piano Concerto no. 4)	Beethoven (Claudio Arrau, piano; Royal Concertgebouw Orchestra, Amsterdam; Bernard Haitink)	Philips Classics (Universal) 468 113-2	57
61	Allegro spiritoso (Movement 4 from Symphony no. 104)	Haydn (London Philharmonic Orchestra; Sir Georg Solti)	The Decca Record Company Limited 417 330-2	59
62	Allegro Moderato (Movement 1 from Piano Concerto no. 4)	Beethoven (Royal Concertgebouw Orchestra, Amsterdam; Bernard Haitink)	Philips Classics (Universal) 468 113-2	60
63	You Always Hurt Me	Curtis Mayfield and The Impressions	Deutsche Grammophon	63
64	Introduction and Allegro	Maurice Ravel (Nicanor Zabaleta; Monique Frasca-Colombier; Marguerite Vidal; Anka Moraver; Hamisa Dor; Christian Larde; Guy Deplus)	Deutsche Grammophon 463 084-2	64
65	The Earle of Essex Galiard	John Dowland (Rose Consort of Viols; Jacob Heringman)	Naxos 8.553326	65

CD track	Title	Composer *(Performers)*	Recording Co.	Page
66	**Allegro Molto Moderato** (Movement 1 from Symphony no. 6)	**Jean Sibelius** *(Berlin Philharmonic Orchestra; Herbert von Karajan)*	Deutsche Grammophon **474 353-2**	65
67	**Aria: 'Endlich, endlich wird mein Joch'** from Cantata no. 56	**J S Bach** *(Thomas Quasthoff (bass-baritone); Berliner Barock Solisten; Rainer Kussmaul)*	Deutsche Grammophon **474 505-2**	66
68	**Largo (Trio)** (from *Pulcinella*)	**Igor Stravinsky** *(London Symphony Orchestra; Claudio Abbado)*	Deutsche Grammophon **453 085-2**	67
69	**Adagio** (from Violin Concerto no. 5)	**Vieuxtemps** *(Chee-Yun; London Philharmonic Orchestra)*	Union Square Music Ltd **SIMPLYCD003-1**	68
70	**Rondo** (Movement 3 from Piano Concerto no. 4)	**Beethoven** *(Claudio Arrau, piano; Royal Concertgebouw Orchestra Amsterdam; Bernard Haitink)*	Philips Classics (Universal) **468 113-2**	68

Acknowledgements

Thanks to everyone at Hodder Gibson.

The Publishers would like to thank the following for permission to reproduce copyright material:

1 Beethoven: Movement 3 Adadgio molto e cantabile (Symphony No.9 in D minor, Op.125), Performed by Berliner Philharmoniker, Courtesy of Deutsche Grammophon under licence from Universal Music Operations; 2 Joe McGowan: 'Exsamplin", Performed by Joe McGowan; 3 Schubert: Kriegers Ahnung (from Schwanengesang), Performed by Peter Schreier, Courtesy of The Decca Record Company Limited under licence from Universal Music Operations; 4 Armath and J Deja: 'We Are the Champ', Performed by Joe McGowan; 5 Beethoven: Movement 1 Allegro moderato (Piano Concerto No.4 in G, Op.58), Performed by Royal Concertgebouw Orchestra, Courtesy of Philips Classics under licence from Universal Music Operations; 6 John Green: 'Body and Soul', Performed by Joe McGowan; 7 Haydn: Movement 1 Adagio - Allegro (Symphony in D, H.I No.104), Performed by London Philharmonic Orchestra, Courtesy of The Decca Record Company Limited under licence from Universal Music Operations; 8 Beethoven: Movement 1 Allegro ma non troppo (Symphony No. 9 in D Minor), Performed by Berliner Philharmoniker, Courtesy of Deutsche Grammophon under licence from Universal Music Operations; 9 Mozart: Movement 2 Adagio, from Clarinet Concerto in A Major K622, from the album, Mozart: Wind Concertos, AV0035, Used by permission of AVIE Records; 10 Charles Ives: Adagio Cantabile (movement 3 from Symphony No 2), Licensed courtesy of Naxos Rights International; 11 Haydn: Movement 7 Arie – Rollend in schäumenden Wellen, Performed by Gerald Finley, Courtesy of Archiv Produktion under licence from Universal Music Operations; 12 Stravinsky: Movement 10 Largo (Trio) 'Sento dire no'ncè pace', Performed by London Symphony Orchestra, Courtesy of Deutsche Grammophon under licence from Universal Music Operations; 13 Dowland: All ye whom love or fortune, Licensed courtesy of Naxos Rights International; 14 'Vezzosi augelli', Performed by G. Wert, from the album 'Italian Madrigals', Used by kind permission of Pickwick Group Limited; 15 Dowland: Mr John Langton's Pavan, Licensed courtesy of Naxos Rights International; 16 Morley: Now is the Month of Maying, Licensed courtesy of Naxos Rights International; 17 Palestrina: Agnus Dei II, Mass for Pentecost, Used by permission of Nimbus Records; 18 Dowland: The King of Denmark's Galliard, Licensed courtesy of Naxos Rights International; 20 Palestrina: Motet – Dum complerentur dies pentecostes, Used by permission of Nimbus Records; 21 Minuetto Vivace (Concerto Grosso in C, op 6, no. 10, Performed by The English Concert, Courtesy of Archiv Produktion under licence from Universal Music Operations; 22 J.S. Bach: Movement 3 Choral – O große Lieb, o Lieb ohn' alle Maße, performed by English Baroque Soloists, Courtesy of Polydor Records under licence from Universal Music Operations; 23 J.S. Bach: Overture No.4 In D Bwv 1069, Performed by Trevor Pinnock, Courtesy of Deutsche Grammophon under licence from Universal Music Operations; 24 J.S. Bach: Das alte Jahr vergangen ist BWV 1091, Licensed by kind permission of BIS Records; 25 J.S. Bach: Movement 5 Menuet (Suite No.1 in C, BWV 1066), Performed by The English Concert, Courtesy of Deutsche Grammophon under licence from Universal Music Operations; 26 J S Bach: Fugue No. 19 in A Major BWV 864, Licensed courtesy of Naxos Rights International; 27 J S Bach: Canon 4. a 2 per Augmentation contrario motu, Licensed courtesy of Naxos Rights International; 28 Vivaldi: Allegro ('Spring'

from The Four Seasons), Used by permission of Union Square Music Ltd.; 29 Handel: 'Praise the Lord' (Solomon HWV 67 / Act 3), Performed by English Baroque Soloists, Courtesy of Philips Classics under licence from Universal Music Operations; 30 Handel: Zadok the Priest (Coronation Anthem No.1, HWV 258), Performed by The Academy of St. Martin in the Fields, Courtesy of Philips Classics under licence from Universal Music Operations; 31 Mozart: Piano sonata no.15 in C major, K545, movement 1, Allegro, Licensed courtesy of Naxos Rights International; 32 Mozart – Trio No. 7 for Piano, Violin and Cello – 1st Movement, Used by permission of Chandos Records Limited; 33 Mozart – Trio No. 7 for Piano, Violin and Cello – 1st Movement, Used by permission of Chandos Records Limited; 34 Beethoven: Movement 2 Molto vivace (Symphony No.9 in D minor, Op.125), Performed by Berliner Philharmoniker, Courtesy of Deutsche Grammophon under licence from Universal Music Operations; 35 Debussy: L'apres Midi, Licensed courtesy of Naxos Rights International; 36 Eric Satie: Gnossienne, Used by permission of Union Square Music Ltd.; 37 Mozart: 'Il capro e la capretta' (Le nozze di Figaro, K.492 / Act 4), Performed by English Baroque Soloists, Courtesy of Archiv Produktion under licence from Universal Music Operations; 38 Beethoven: Movement 1 Allegro moderato (Piano Concerto No.4 in G, Op.58), Performed by Royal Concertgebouw Orchestra, Courtesy of Philips Classics under licence from Universal Music Operations; 39 Wagner: 'Isolde! Geliebte! - Tristan! Geliebter! (Tristan und Isolde / Act 2), Performed by Staatskapelle Dresden, Courtesy of Deutsche Grammophon under licence from Universal Music Operations; 40 Schubert: Das Fischermädchen (Schwanengesang), Performed by Peter Schreier, Courtesy of The Decca Record Company Limited under licence from Universal Music Operations; 41 Tchaikovsky: Romeo and Juliet Fantasy Overture, from the album Best of Classics, released by DGR Records; 42 Dvorak: Slavonic Dance in C Major, op 46, no 1, from the album Best of Classics, released by DGR Records; 43 Saint-Saëns: 'Aquarium [Carnaval des Animaux)', Performed by Martha Argerich, Courtesy of Deutsche Grammophon under licence from Universal Music Operations; 44 Saint-Saëns: Movement 3 Maestoso - Allegro (Symphony No.3 in C minor, Op.78), Performed by Orchestre de l'Opéra Bastille, Courtesy of Deutsche Grammophon under licence from Universal Music Operations; 45 Sibelius: Movement 1 Allegro molto moderato (Symphony No.6 in D minor, Op.104), Performed by Berliner Philharmoniker, Courtesy of Deutsche Grammophon under licence from Universal Music Operations; 46 Glass: Movement 3 (Concerto for Violin and Orchestra), Performed by Wiener Philharmoniker, Courtesy of Deutsche Grammophon under licence from Universal Music Operations; 47 Stockhausen: Explosion 1, Licensed by kind permission of BIS Records; 48 CD Inde Du Nord/North India – Pandit Ravi Shankar – C 581674 – Ocora Radio France; 49 Charles Ives: Symphony No. 2 – IV. Lento Maestoso, Licensed courtesy of Naxos Rights International; 50 Schoenberg: Einziger, ewiger, allgegenwärtiger, Performed by David Pittmann-Jennings, Courtesy of Deutsche Grammophon under licence from Universal Music Operations; 51 Charles Ives: 'The Gong on the Hook and Ladder' (or 'Fireman's Parade on Main Street'), Performed by Ensemble Modern, Courtesy of EMI Records Limited; 52 Sally Oldfield: 'Flaming Star', Performed by Sally Oldfield, Courtesy of New World Music, Harmony House, Hillside Road East, Bungay, Suffolk, NR35 1RX, www.newworldmusic.com; 53 'Bendrong' (Traditional), from the album 'Flute and gamelan music of West Java', Courtesy of Topic Records Ltd., www.topicrecords.co.uk; 54 Charles Ives: Central Park in the Dark, Performed by The Gulbenkian Orchestra, Used by permission of Nimbus Records; 55 Beethoven: Movement 1 Allegro moderato [Piano Concerto No.4 in G, Op.58), Performed by Royal Concertgebouw Orchestra, Courtesy of Philips Classics under licence from Universal